FOREWORD   The New ICC Guide to Documentary Credits, ICC Publication No. 515, is a revision of the ICC Guide to Documentary Credits, ICC Publication No. 415. This new guide reflects the changes introduced by the 1993 revision of the UCP 500 and the new ICC Publication No. 516, Standard Documentary Credit Forms (1993 revision).

International trade involves a flow of goods from seller to buyer in accordance with a contract of sale. Similarly, after the goods have been supplied there must be a flow of payment from the buyer to the seller. Usually, the parties in international trade are aware that such payment may be influenced by various issues, such as trust between the commercial parties, their need for finance and, possibly, by governmental trade and exchange control regulations.

While there are various methods of settling international trade transactions, one of the most common methods of payment is the Documentary Credit. Since 1933, when the International Chamber of Commerce first published The Uniform Customs and Practice for Documentary Credits, the ICC has considered it important to keep the business community abreast of developments and practices that have evolved in this field, and to support efforts to facilitate and standardise international trade practices. Accordingly, the ICC offers this publication as an educational tool, and trusts that the commercial parties, bankers and business students worldwide will benefit from these pages.

Charles del Busto
Chairman
ICC Commission on Banking Technique and Practice
January 1, 1994

Table of Contents

I. General Introduction

1. International Trade Considerations

While this publication is devoted mainly to Documentary Credits, it is important for the various parties engaged in international trade to have a general understanding of some of the basic political, legal and economic issues that make up the framework within which such trade takes place. For this reason, the first part of the book is devoted to a discussion of those basic issues, which should also help the reader appreciate the benefits of the Documentary Credit when compared to other means of payment used in trade transactions.

Prior to that discussion, one must acknowledge a general principle, namely, that in every international trade transaction there must be:

a seller

an agreed product or service

a sales contract

shipping and delivery details

a buyer

terms of payment

required documentation

insurance cover

2. A List of Political, Legal and Economic Issues to be Considered in International Trade

Before entering into an international trade transaction, the parties should take account of the political, legal and economic framework within which their transaction will be taking place. This means they should consider the following:

Political / governmental policies and their potential impact on the transaction

These include:

- restrictive governmental policies,
- exchange controls,
- tariffs and quota restrictions,
- expropriation,
- export/import licensing,
- trade embargoes,
- anti-dumping legislation,
- pre-shipment inspection/price comparisons,
- resale price restrictions,
- health requirements,
- policies on hazardous goods, and
- taxation.

Currency policies of the importing and exporting countries: the risks associated with them and the parties' ability to comply with them

These include:

- foreign exchange policies and procedures,
- licensing,
- scarcity of convertible currency,
- fluctuation or volatility of exchange rates, and
- covering and hedging of foreign exchange exposure.

Fraud possibilities in the transaction or in documents

Payment against documents for imports en route cannot give protection against the risk of fraud when dealing with a seller who is not known, or concerning whom reports are not wholly satisfactory.
"Know who" can be even more important than "know how".
Furthermore, goods should not be shipped or a service provided merely against a "paper promise to pay" which has not been thoroughly examined, authenticated or verified.

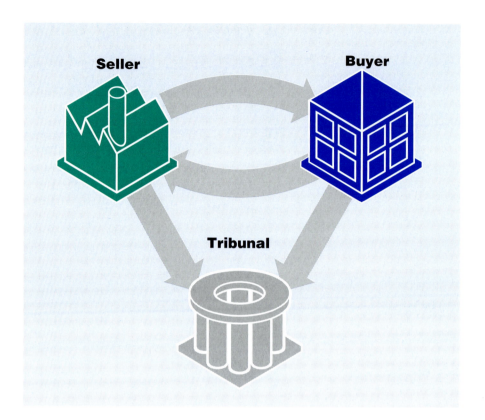

Jurisdictional and other legal issues that should be considered

Dispute settlement
- locale of contract's enforcement,
- availability of legal representation, and
- legal policies towards foreign corporations.

Legal requirements
- as to the quality of the goods or services to be performed,
- as to the specification of the goods or services,
- as to the labelling,
- as to the packaging/marking of the goods, and
- as to retention of title to the goods.

Intellectual property rights
- registry of trade marks, patents or copyrights, both domestic and international.

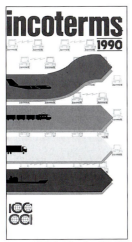

ICC Publication N° 460

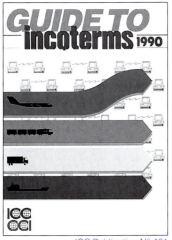

ICC Publication N° 461

Trade terms or shipping terms in international trade

Trade terms are one of the key elements of international contracts of sale. They identify for the parties what to do with respect to their individual responsibilities.

Shipping goods from one country to another under a commercial transaction has its risks. If upon formalising a contract of sale, the buyer and the seller specifically incorporate one of the trade terms used in international commerce, they may be assured that they have defined their respective responsibilities in a simple and secure manner. This should eliminate any possibility of misinterpretation and any corresponding disputes.

In the 1920s, the International Chamber of Commerce conducted a study on the interpretation of the more important trade terms. This study demonstrated that the terms were understood differently in different countries. Therefore, the outcome of a dispute between the seller and buyer often depended on the place where the dispute would be resolved and the applicable law. This, of course, involved judicial risks for the seller or the buyer which could create serious disputes and adversely affect future business between them.

For this reason, the International Chamber of Commerce considered it important to develop rules for the interpretation of trade terms which the parties to the contract of sale could agree to apply - INCOTERMS - for international commercial terms . These rules were first published in 1936.

The principal trade terms normally utilised in international trade are the INCOTERMS 1990. They are normally applicable:

- by reference in the contract of sale,
- as an international custom of the trade, and
- by assuming that the parties have intended to apply them (so-called implication).

3. Documentary Requirements

Commercial and financial documentary requirements

The parties to the international trade transaction must address the following documentary issues:

Buyer

what document(s) does the buyer need?

Seller

what document(s) will he be able to supply?

Country of export

what documents are required under the regulations of the exporting country? and

Country of import

what documents are required under the regulations of the importing country?

4. Main Objectives of the Parties to a Transaction

The buyer's objectives are:

Contract fulfilment

- ■ To receive the correct quantity and quality of the goods purchased or services required,
- ■ To receive, in a timely manner and at the correct place, the goods purchased or the services required, and
- ■ Assurance that he does not have to pay the seller until he is certain that the seller has fulfilled his obligations correctly.

Credit

- ■ A managed cash flow, with the possibility of obtaining bank finance, and/or
- ■ To defer payment as long as possible.

Convenience

- ■ The convenience of using an intervening third party in whom both the buyer and the seller have confidence - such as a bank with its Documentary Credit expertise - when payment is to be made.

The seller's objectives are:

Contract fulfilment

- ■ Assurance that he will be paid in full within the agreed time limit, and
- ■ To deliver the contracted goods or services as quickly as possible.

Prompt payment

- ■ Prompt payment on completion of his contractual obligation, so as to improve the liquidity of his business, and
- ■ To receive payment of the correct amount and in the correct currency.

Convenience

- ■ The convenience of receiving payment at his own bank or through a bank in his own country.

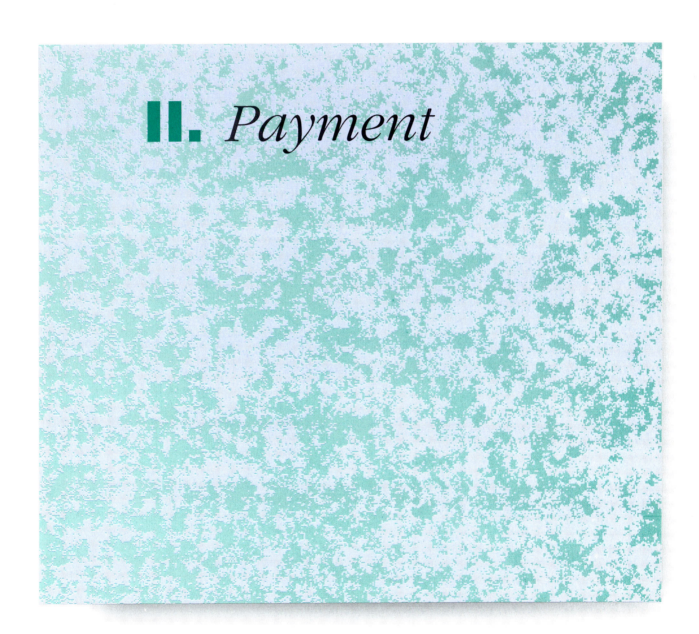

II. *Payment*

1. Payment Considerations

For the seller

In advance

He needs payment since he cannot otherwise finance the production of the goods and/or services the buyer has ordered.

At time of shipment or rendering of services

He wants assurance of payment as soon as the goods are shipped or the services are rendered.

After shipment or rendering of services

He is prepared to wait for payment for a certain time after shipment or after the services are rendered, since he trusts the buyer and appreciates his position.

For the buyer

In advance

He trusts the seller, knowing that the contract will be carried out as agreed, and he is therefore prepared to pay in advance.

At time of shipment or rendering of services

He does not want to take the risk of paying before being certain that the goods are shipped on time or that the services are rendered and that they are as stipulated in his contract with the seller.

After shipment or rendering of services

He possibly wants to sell the goods or to be satisfied that the services have been rendered before he pays the seller.

2. Means of Payment

The following categories are the usual methods of payment to settle international trade transactions:

Cash in advance

☞ **Definition**

The buyer places the funds at the disposal of the seller prior to shipment of the goods or provision of services.

While this method of payment is expensive and contains degrees of risk, it is not uncommon when the manufacturing process or services delivered are specialised and capital intensive. In such circumstances the parties may agree to fund the operation by partial payments in advance or by progress payments.

This method of payment is used:

- when the buyer's credit is doubtful,
- when there is an unstable political or economic environment in the buyer's country, and/or
- if there is a potential delay in the receipt of funds from the buyer, perhaps due to events beyond his control.

Advantages to the seller
- immediate use of funds.

Disadvantages to the buyer
- He pays in advance, tying up his capital prior to receipt of the goods or services,
- He has no assurance that what he contracted for will be:
  - supplied,
  - received,
  - received in a timely fashion, and/or,
  - received in the quality or quantity ordered.

Open account

☞ **Definition**

An arrangement between the buyer and seller whereby the goods are manufactured and delivered before payment is required.

Open account provides for payment at some stated specific future date and without the buyer issuing any negotiable instrument evidencing his legal commitment. The seller must have absolute trust that he will be paid at the agreed date. The seller should recognise that in certain instances it is possible to discount open accounts receivable with a financial institution.

Advantages to the buyer

- He pays for the goods or services only when they are received and/or inspected, and
- Payment is conditioned on the issues discussed in the previous chapter, "A List of the Political, Legal and Economic Issues to be Considered in International Trade".

Disadvantages to the seller

- He releases the title to the goods without having assurance of payment,
- There is a possibility that political events will impose regulations which defer or block the movement of funds to him, and
- His own capital is tied up until the goods are received and/or inspected by the buyer or until the services are found to be acceptable and payment is made.

Collection

Definition

An arrangement whereby the goods are shipped and the relevant bill of exchange (Draft) is drawn by the seller on the buyer, and/or document(s) is sent to the seller's bank with clear instructions for collection through one of its correspondent bank located in the domicile of the buyer.

Normally, title to the goods does not pass to the buyer (unless the buyer is the named consignee on the transport document) until the Draft is paid or accepted by the buyer. Collections provide the parties with an alternative arrangement other than open account or cash in advance. Collections are usually connected with the sale of goods rather than with the provision of services.

Normal precautions to be taken by the seller

The seller should:

- obtain a credit report on the buyer,
- obtain an economic and political analysis on the country of importation,
- not consign the goods to the buyer and not consign the goods to the buyer's bank (the Collecting Bank) without that bank's prior agreement, and
- establish alternative procedures for the resale, reshipment or warehousing of the goods in the event of non-payment by the buyer.

1. Documentary Collection

- The seller ships the goods and obtains the shipping documents and usually draws a Draft, either at sight or with a tenor of x days, on the buyer for the value of the goods,
- The seller submits the Draft(s) and/or document(s) to his bank which acts as his agent (the Remitting Bank). The bank acknowledges that all documents as noted by the seller are presented,
- The seller's bank (the Remitting Bank) sends the Draft and the other documents along with a collection letter to a correspondent bank (the Collecting Bank) usually located in the same city as the buyer,
- Acting as an agent for the Remitting Bank, the Collecting Bank notifies the buyer upon receipt of the Draft and documents, and
- All the documents, and usually title to the goods, are released to the buyer upon his payment of the amount specified or his acceptance of the Draft for payment at a specified later date.

Advantages to the seller

- Documentary collections are uncomplicated and inexpensive,
- Documents of value, i.e. title documents, are not released to the buyer until payment or acceptance has been effected. In the event of non-payment or non-acceptance, the Collecting Bank, if properly authorised, may arrange for the goods release, warehousing, insurance or even re-shipment to the seller, and
- Collections may facilitate pre-export or post-export financing.

Disadvantages to the seller

- He ships the goods without an unconditional promise of payment by the buyer,
- There is no guarantee of payment or immediate payment by the buyer, and
- He ties up his capital until the funds are received.

Advantages for the buyer

- Collections may favour the buyer since payment is deferred by him until the goods arrive or even later if delayed payment arrangements are agreed to.

Disadvantages to the buyer

- By defaulting on a bill of exchange he may become legally liable, and
- His trade reputation may be damaged if the collection remains unpaid.

2. Clean Collection

An arrangement whereby the seller draws only a Draft on the buyer for the value of the goods/services and presents the Draft to his bank.

The seller's bank (the Remitting Bank) sends the Draft along with a collection instruction letter to a correspondent bank (the Collecting Bank) usually in the same city as the buyer.

A clean collection may represent:

■ an underlying merchandise transaction, or
■ an underlying financial transaction.

3. Direct Collection

An arrangement whereby the seller obtains his bank's pre-numbered direct collection letter, thus enabling him to send his documents directly to his bank's correspondent bank for collection. This kind of collection accelerates the paperwork process.

The seller forwards to his bank (the Remitting Bank) a copy of the respective instruction/collection letter that has been forwarded directly by him to the correspondent bank (the Collecting Bank). The Remitting Bank treats this transaction in the same fashion as a normal documentary collection item, as if it were completely processed by such Remitting Bank.

Documentary Credit

 Definition

The Documentary Credit or letter of credit is an undertaking issued by a bank for the account of the buyer (the Applicant) or for its own account, to pay the Beneficiary the value of the Draft and/or documents provided that the terms and conditions of the Documentary Credit are complied with.

This Documentary Credit arrangement usually satisfies the seller's desire for cash and the importer's desire for credit. This financial instrument serves the interest of both parties independently. The Documentary Credit offers a unique and universally used method of achieving a commercially acceptable undertaking by providing for payment to be made against complying documents that represent the goods and making possible the transfer of title to those goods.

Unfortunately, fraudulent Documentary Credits issued by a fictitious non-existing "bank" are a fact of life. In some instances, the "Beneficiary" receives the Documentary Credit direct from some such "bank", i.e. without the intervention of a known Advising Bank in the Beneficiary's country, which Advising Bank may be able to check the apparent authenticity of the "Documentary Credit". This departure from normal banking routine can signal danger. In other instances, the Advising Bank purports to be a branch or office of the "Issuing Bank" but is an unknown name so far as the Beneficiary is concerned. This, too, can signal the need for caution. In all cases the safeguard is for the "Beneficiary" to check with his own bank before relying, or acting, on the "Documentary Credit".

For a further detailed explanation of the definition of a Documentary Credit, refer to **UCP 500 Article 2**.

Contractual arrangements

Under a Documentary Credit operation, there exists a distinct triangular contractual arrangement:

- First, the sales contract between buyer and seller,
- Second, the "Application and Security Agreement" or the "Reimbursing Agreement" between the buyer (the Applicant) and the issuer (the Issuing Bank), and
- Third, the Documentary Credit between the Issuing Bank and the Beneficiary. If the Documentary Credit is confirmed by another bank, then such bank undertakes its own contractual arrangement, in addition to that of the Issuing Bank, to the Beneficiary.

Each contract is independent and controls the respective relationship between the parties. The **UCP 500 in sub-Article 3(a)** recognises that relationship and states:

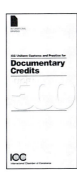

"*Credits, by their nature, are separate transactions from the sales or other contract(s) on which they may be based, and banks are in no way concerned with or bound by such contract(s), even if any reference whatsoever to such contract(s) is included in the Credit. Consequently, the undertaking of a bank to pay, accept and pay Draft(s) or negotiate and/or to fulfil any other obligation under the Credit is not subject to claims or defences by the Applicant resulting from his relationships with the Issuing Bank or the Beneficiary.*"

And **UCP 500 sub-Article 3(b)** states:

"*A Beneficiary can in no case avail himself of the contractual relationships existing between the banks or between the Applicant and the Issuing Bank.*"

Issuing a Documentary Credit

1.

The buyer and the seller conclude a sales contract providing for payment by Documentary Credit

2.

The buyer instructs his bank - the "Issuing" Bank - to issue a Credit in favour of the seller (Beneficiary)

3.

The Issuing Bank asks another bank, usually in the country of the seller, to advise and perhaps also to add its confirmation to the Documentary Credit

4.

The Advising or Confirming Bank informs the seller that the Credit has been issued

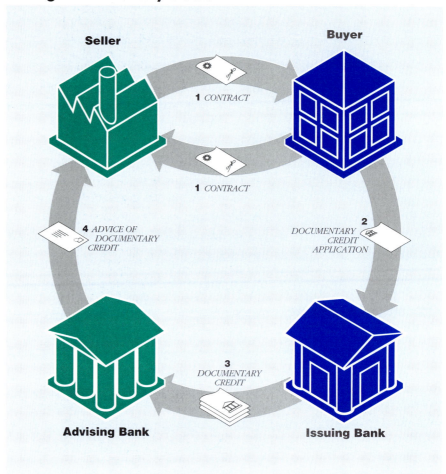

Parties to a Documentary Credit

The parties are:
- the Issuing Bank,
- the Confirming Bank, if any, and
- the Beneficiary.

Other parties which facilitate the Documentary Credit are:
- the Applicant,
- the Advising Bank,
- the Nominated Paying/Negotiating/Accepting Bank, and
- the Transferring Bank, if any.

Benefits of the Documentary Credit

Facilitates financing

The Documentary Credit:
- provides a specific transaction with an independent credit backing and a clear cut promise of payment,
- satisfies the financing needs of the seller and the buyer by placing the bank's credit standing, distinguished from the bank's funds, at the disposal of both parties,
- may allow the buyer to obtain a lower purchase price for the goods as well as longer payment terms than would open account terms, or a collection,
- reduces or eliminates the commercial credit risk since payment is assured by the bank which issues an irrevocable Documentary Credit. The seller no longer needs to rely on the willingness and capability of the buyer to make payment,
- reduces certain exchange and political risks while not necessarily eliminating them,
- may not require actual segregation of cash, since the buyer is not always required to collateralise his Documentary Credit obligation to the Issuing Bank, and
- expands sources of supply for the buyers since certain sellers are willing to sell only against cash in advance or a Documentary Credit.

Provides legal protection

Documentary Credits are supported by a wide variety of laws and regulations such as:
- legislative and semi-legislative law,
- codified law - in most countries the law for Documentary Credits has been codified, e.g. in
  - civil law code countries, and in
  - common law code countries
- decisional law - statutory laws governing Documentary Credits are found in various jurisdictions. There are also extensive legal cases that have interpreted these statutory provisions and are well known in judicial circles,
- contractual law/customary law - in addition to codified and case law, Documentary Credits are usually governed by the International Chamber of Commerce's, Uniform Customs and Practices for Documentary Credits. These rules, which are periodically revised, have been in effect since 1933 and are the set of universally recognised rules governing Documentary Credit operations.

The UCP rules are adopted by banks through collective notification to the International Chamber of Commerce, by the respective National Committees of the ICC, by the national banking association of the country, by a bank's individual adherence and notification to the ICC, or by incorporation of the UCP in the Documentary Credit itself.

Assures expert examination of documents

- The buyer is assured that the documents required by the Documentary Credit (if issued subject to the UCP) must be presented in compliance with the terms and conditions of the Documentary Credit and the UCP rules,
- The buyer is assured that the documents presented will be examined by banking personnel knowledgeable in Documentary Credit operations, and
- The buyer is confident that payment will only be made to the seller after the terms and conditions of the Documentary Credit and the UCP rules are complied with.

Summary of Documentary Credits

The Documentary Credit:
- is a facility provided by banks in order to facilitate international trade transactions,
- assures all the contracting parties that the Issuing Bank or a Confirming Bank, if any, will honour its obligation provided the terms and conditions of the Documentary Credit are complied with,
- assures payment, as long as the terms and conditions of the Documentary Credit are complied with,
- assures payment on the basis of documents alone and not based on the goods or services to which it may refer.

However, it is worth repeating that prior to establishing commercial relations, it is important that the buyer inform himself about the financial and business reputation of the seller.

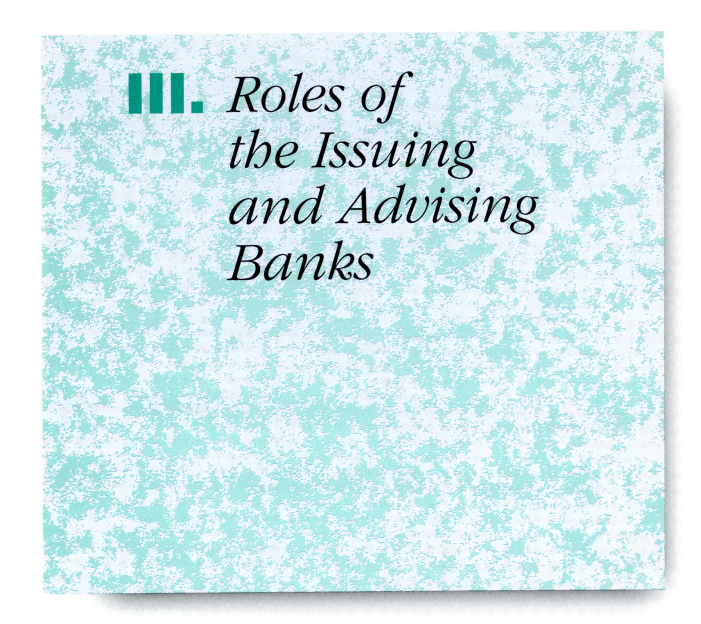

III. Roles of the Issuing and Advising Banks

There are usually two banks involved in a Documentary Credit operation. The Issuing Bank is the bank acting for and on behalf of the buyer. The Advising Bank is a bank chosen to advise the Documentary Credit to the Beneficiary and is usually located in the seller's country.

This second bank can be simply an Advising Bank, or it can also assume the more important role of a Confirming Bank. In either case, the Advising Bank can undertake the transmission of the Documentary Credit. The Uniform Customs and Practices for Documentary Credits, **UCP 500**, states in **sub-Article 7(a)**: "A Credit may be advised to a Beneficiary through another bank (the Advising Bank) without engagement on the part of the Advising Bank, but that bank, if it elects to advise the Credit, shall take reasonable care to check the apparent authenticity of the Credit which it advises..."

If the second bank is simply "advising the Credit" without any obligation on its part, it will mention this fact when it forwards the Documentary Credit to the seller (the Beneficiary). Such a bank is under no commitment to make payment, incur a deferred payment undertaking, accept Draft(s) or negotiate, even though it may be nominated in the Documentary Credit as the bank authorised to pay, to accept, or to negotiate. (See **UCP 500 sub-Article 10(c)**).

If the Advising Bank has been authorised or requested by the Issuing Bank to add its confirmation and it is prepared to do so, it will state accordingly on its advice to the Beneficiary. This means that the Confirming Bank, effectively in a separate banking contract with the Beneficiary and regardless of any other consideration, must pay, accept, or negotiate without recourse to the Beneficiary, provided all the documents stipulated in the Documentary Credit are presented in order and that the terms and conditions of the Documentary Credit are complied with (See **UCP 500 sub-Article 9(b)**).

Stages to a Documentary Credit

The New **Standard Documentary Credit Forms** *for the UCP 500*

Edited by Charles del Busto

International Chamber of Commerce

ICC Publication N° 516

Documentary Credit Application

For a detailed explanation of the ICC's recommended execution of the Documentary Credit Application, all parties should refer to ICC Publication No. 516, which provides a number of recommended Standard Forms and full information about how to complete them. The Application should include, amongst other details, the following:

(1) the full (and correct) name and address of the Beneficiary (seller),

(2) the amount of the Documentary Credit and its ISO Currency Code,

(3) the type of Documentary Credit, whether

- revocable,
- irrevocable, or
- irrevocable, with the added information that the Nominated Bank is requested or authorised to add its confirmation to the Documentary Credit.

(4) how the Documentary Credit is to be available, e.g. by payment, deferred payment, acceptance, or negotiation,

(5) the party on whom Draft(s), if any, are to be drawn and the tenor of such Draft(s),

(6) a brief description of the goods, including details of quantity and unit price, if any,

(7) details of the documents required,

(8) the place where the goods are to be dispatched, taken in charge, or loaded on board, as the case may be, and the place of final destination, or the port of discharge,

(9) whether freight is to be prepaid or not,

(10) whether transhipment is prohibited or not,

(11) whether part shipments are prohibited or not,

(12) the last date for shipment (if applicable),

(13) the period of time after the date of shipment within which the documents must be presented for payment, acceptance, or negotiation,

(14) the date and place of expiry of the Documentary Credit,

(15) whether or not the Documentary Credit is to be a Transferable Credit,

(16) how the Documentary Credit is to be advised, i.e., by mail or by teletransmission.

N.B. Some of the above are not applicable when the Documentary Credit is to cover payment of services.

Irrevocable Documentary Credit Application

(3) Irrevocable Documentary Credit Application

Applicant:	Issuing Bank:

Date of Application:

☐ Issue by (air) mail   ☐ with brief advice by teletransmission (see UCP 500 Article 11) **(16)**

☐ Issue by teletransmission (see UCP 500 Article 11)

☐ Transferable Credit-as per UCP 500 Article 48 **(15)**

Expiry Date and Place for Presentation of Documents **(14)**
Expiry Date:

Place for Presentation:

Beneficiary: **(1)**

Confirmation of the Credit: **(3)**

☐ not requested   ☐ requested   ☐ authorised if requested by Beneficiary

Amount in figures and words (Please use ISO Currency Codes): **(2)**

Partial shipments ☐ allowed ☐ not allowed **(11)**

Transhipments ☐ allowed ☐ not allowed **(10)**

Please refer to UCP 500 transport Articles for exceptions to this condition

☐ Insurance will be covered by us

Credit available with Nominated Bank: **(4)**

☐ by payment at sight

☐ by deferred payment at:

☐ by acceptance of drafts at:

☐ by negotiation:

Shipment as defined in UCP 500 Article 46 **(8)**
From:

For transportation to:

Not later than: **(12)**

Against the documents detailed herein:

☐ and Beneficiary's draft(s) drawn on: **(5)**

Goods (Brief description without excessive details - See UCP 500 Article 5): **(6)**

Terms: **(6)**

☐ FAS   ☐ CIF

☐ FOB   ☐ Other terms:

☐ CFR   ☐ as per INCOTERMS

Commercial invoice ☐ signed, original and ☐ copies.

Transport Document: **(7)**
☐ Multimodal Transport Document, covering at least two different modes of transport
☐ Marine/Ocean Bill of Lading covering a port-to-port shipment
☐ Non-Negotiable Sea Waybill covering a port-to-port shipment
☐ Air Waybill, original for the consignor
☐ Other transport document:
☐ to the order of
☐ endorsed in blank
☐ marked freight ☐ prepaid ☐ payable at destination **(9)**
☐ notify:

Insurance Document:
☐ Policy ☐ Certificate ☐ Declaration under an open cover. Covering the following risks:

Certificates:
☐ Origin
☐ Analysis
☐ Health
☐ Other

Other Documents:
☐ Packing List
☐ Weight List

Documents to be presented within ☐ days after the date of shipment but within the validity of the Credit. **(13)**

(3)

Additional Instructions:

We request you to issue on our behalf and for our account your Irrevocable Credit in accordance with the above instructions (marked (x) where appropriate).
This Credit will be subject to the Uniform Customs and Practice for Documentary Credits (1993 Revision, Publication No. 500 of the International Chamber of Commerce, Paris, France), insofar as they are applicable.

Name and signature of the Applicant

Consult the Issuing Bank for guidance if the completion of this form should raise any question

Review of the Documentary Credit Application and security agreement by the Issuing Bank

The Issuing Bank should:

- review the terms and conditions of the proposed Documentary Credit to ensure that they are in compliance with the policies of the bank and in accordance with the legal requirements or regulations of the Issuing Bank's country, and
- review whether the Applicant's instructions, as to the method of notifying the Beneficiary, are acceptable or whether the bank is authorised to choose its own correspondent for advising the Documentary Credit.

Applicants, at times, request the issuance of Documentary Credits containing excessive details for the Beneficiary to comply with under the Documentary Credit. Unfortunately, banks appear to be reluctant to discourage this practice. There is some concern that certain Applicants include excessive details with the intention that the Beneficiary may overlook certain conditions or present documents with discrepancies which would cause the documents to be refused if the Applicant so desired.

Moreover, the Issuing Bank should carefully review the Documentary Credit Application to determine if the Documentary Credit would require the Beneficiary to submit a document, the performance or production of which is totally dependent on the performance by a third party not controlled by the Beneficiary (other than a transport document, an insurance document or an inspection certificate etc.). In addition, the Issuing Bank should also carefully review the Documentary Credit Application to determine that there are no "nondocumentary conditions" stated in the Application. If there are such conditions, it is the responsibility of the Issuing Bank to inform the Applicant that these conditions must be transformed into a distinct documentary requirement. (See **UCP 500 sub-Article 13 (c)**)

Utilisation of the Documentary Credit

Upon receipt of the Documentary Credit, the Beneficiary should review it to see that:

- the Documentary Credit appears to be a valid Documentary Credit,
- the type of Documentary Credit and its terms and conditions are in accordance with the sales contract,
- the Documentary Credit does not contain any conditions which are unacceptable or impossible to comply with,
- the documents required by the Documentary Credit are obtainable and presentable under the Documentary Credit,
- the goods description or unit prices, if any, are as stated in the sales contract,
- there are no conditions indicated in the Documentary Credit requiring payment of interest, charges, or expenses not contracted for in the sales contract,
- the shipping and expiry dates indicated in the Documentary Credit and the period for presentation of the documents are sufficient to enable the Beneficiary to comply with them in order to obtain payment thereunder,
- the port of loading, taking in charge, or place of dispatch and the port of discharge or delivery correspond to the sales contract,
- the insurance requirement (whether is to be covered by the Beneficiary or the buyer) is declared in the Documentary Credit, and
- the bank's obligation under the Documentary Credit is conditioned on total compliance with its terms and conditions and subject to the Uniform Customs and Practices for Documentary Credits, **ICC Publication No. 500**.

Common sense rules for the Beneficiary

(a) Although considerable time may elapse between the receipt of a Documentary Credit and its utilisation, the Beneficiary should not delay studying it immediately and requesting any necessary changes at that time,

(b) The Beneficiary should assure himself that his company's name and address details are exactly as they appear in the Documentary Credit,

(c) A Documentary Credit should always describe, in a very clear and definitive manner, the documents that the Beneficiary must present to obtain payment. A Documentary Credit should not be issued if it declares a condition which is not supported by the presentation of a stated document(s), and

(d) The Beneficiary should satisfy himself that the terms, conditions and documents called for in the Documentary Credit are in agreement with the sales contract,

(e) When making presentation of the documents to the bank, the Beneficiary should:

- present the required documents exactly as called for by the Documentary Credit. They must be in accordance with the terms and conditions of the Documentary Credit and not, on their face, inconsistent with one another,

- present the documents to the bank as quickly as possible, and in any case within the validity of the Documentary Credit and within the period of time after date of shipment specified or applicable under **UCP 500 Article 43**, and

(f) The Beneficiary should remember that non-compliance with the terms and conditions stipulated in the Documentary Credit, or irregularities in the documents, obliges the bank to refuse settlement.

Honouring the obligation under the Documentary Credit

Once the documents have been examined by the bank, which has verified that the terms and conditions of the Documentary Credit have been complied with, delivery of the documents is made by the Confirming Bank to the Issuing Bank and by the Issuing Bank to the Applicant against reimbursement of the sums owed, or against other methods of settlement indicated in the Documentary Credit or the Application.

In certain instances, the documents presented under the Documentary Credit may not comply with its terms and conditions. If so, the bank(s) may only act as follows:

- return the documents to the Beneficiary so that the Beneficiary can correct them and represent them during the period of validity under the Documentary Credit and in accordance with **UCP 500 Article 43**,
- remit under approval, with reference to the Documentary Credit and with the consent of the Beneficiary, the unpaid documents to the respective Issuing Bank or Confirming Bank, if any, for settlement under the Credit,
- return the discrepant documents to the Beneficiary with instructions that he remit the documents directly to the Issuing Bank or Confirming Bank, if any, for their approval and settlement under the Credit,
- request by teletransmission, with the Beneficiary's consent, the Issuing Bank's or Confirming Bank's, if any, authorisation to proceed with the payment, negotiation, or acceptance against the discrepant documents presented,
- require a Beneficiary's guarantee or indemnity or his banker's, undertaking to reimburse the bank for any payment, acceptance, or negotiation it may undertake, despite the fact that the terms and conditions of the Documentary Credit were not complied with if the respective Issuing Bank

or Confirming Bank, if any, refuses to accept such discrepant documents and refuses to reimburse for settlement.

The obligation of the Issuing Bank and the Confirming Bank, if any, is to examine documents in order to determine if there is compliance with the terms and conditions of the Documentary Credit. For this reason it is important to recognise the conditions associated with **UCP 500 Articles 13 and 14** which addresses the standard for examination of documents and the actions to be taken relative to discrepant documents and notice thereof.

IV. *Types and Uses of Documentary Credits*

1 Types

1 *Irrevocable Documentary Credit*

Definition

An irrevocable Documentary Credit constitutes a definite undertaking of the Issuing Bank, provided that the stipulated documents are presented to the Nominated Bank or to the Issuing Bank and that the terms and conditions of the Documentary Credit are complied with, to pay, accept Drafts and/or document(s) presented under the Documentary Credit. (See UCP 500 Article 9, for a full description of the obligations of the Issuing Bank under this kind of Documentary Credit.)

An irrevocable Documentary Credit gives the Beneficiary greater assurance of payment; however, he remains dependent on an undertaking of a foreign Issuing Bank. The Issuing Bank irrevocably commits itself to honour the exporter's Draft and/or documents provided that the stipulated documents are presented and all the stipulations of the Documentary Credit are complied with. The irrevocable Documentary Credit cannot be cancelled/modified without the express consent of the Issuing Bank, the Confirming Bank (if any) and the Beneficiary.

2. *Revocable Documentary Credit*

Definition

A revocable Documentary Credit is issued in favour of the Beneficiary in accordance with the instructions of the Applicant and gives the buyer maximum flexibility, since it can be amended, revoked or cancelled without the Beneficiary's consent and even without prior notice to the Beneficiary up to the moment of payment by the bank at which the Issuing Bank has made the Documentary Credit available.

The revocable Documentary Credit involves risks to the Beneficiary since the Documentary Credit may be amended or cancelled while the goods are in transit and before the documents are presented, or, although documents may have been presented, before payment has been made, or, in the case of a deferred payment Documentary Credit, before documents have been taken up. The seller then faces the problem of obtaining payment directly from the buyer.

The revocable Documentary Credit is normally accepted as usage between affiliated parties or subsidiary companies, or as a usage of a particular trade, or as a substitute for a promise to pay or a payment order.

2. Uses

1. *Irrevocable Straight Documentary Credit*

See page 38

Definition

Under the Irrevocable Straight Documentary Credit, the obligation of the Issuing Bank is extended only to the Beneficiary in honouring Draft(s)/document(s) and usually expires at the counters of the Issuing Bank. This kind of Documentary Credit conveys no commitment or obligation on the part of the Issuing Bank to persons other than the named Beneficiary.

Banks and other financial institutions may elect to purchase the Beneficiary's Drafts/documents. However, the purchaser of a Draft drawn/document presented under such Credit acquires no rights against the Issuing Bank under the Documentary Credit. This kind of Documentary Credit conveys no engagement by the Issuing Bank to protect such purchasers of Drafts/documents. The purchaser of a Draft drawn/documents presented under a straight Documentary Credit only has the right to present the Draft/documents on behalf of the Beneficiary.

The engagement of the Issuing Bank under this kind of Documentary Credit is normally indicated in the Documentary Credit as available for payment by the Issuing Bank and expiring for presentation of documents at the offices of the Issuing Bank. Alternatively, the engagement of the Issuing Bank may be stated more explicitly as follows:

> *"We hereby agree with the Beneficiary that all Drafts drawn under and/or documents presented hereunder will be duly honoured by us provided the terms and conditions of the Credit are complied with **and that presentation is made at this office on or before (the expiry date)",** or words of similar intent.*

Irrevocable Straight Documentary Credit

Name of Issuing Bank: The French Issuing Bank 38 rue François 1er 75008 Paris, France	**Irrevocable Documentary Credit** Number 12345

Place and Date of Issue: Paris, 1 January 1994	**Expiry Date and Place for Presentation of Documents**
Applicant: The French Importer Co. 89 rue du Commerce Paris, France	Expiry Date: May 29, 1994 Place for Presentation: The French Issuing Bank, Paris, France

Beneficiary:
The American Exporter Co. Inc.
17 Main Street
Tampa, Florida

⇐

Advising Bank: Reference. No
The American Advising Bank
456 Commerce Avenue
Tampa, Florida

Amount: US$100,000.- one hundred thousand U.S.Dollars

Partial shipments [X] allowed [ ] not allowed

Transhipment [X] allowed [ ] not allowed

[ ] Insurance covered by buyers

Credit available with Nominated Bank: The French Issuing Bank

[X] by payment at sight

[ ] by deferred payment at:

[ ] by acceptance of drafts at:

[ ] by negotiation

Shipment as defined in UCP 500 Article 46

From: Tampa, Florida

For transportation to: Paris, France

Not later than: May 15, 1994

Against the documents detailed herein:

[X] and Beneficiary's draft(s) drawn on:

The French Issuing Bank, Paris, France

© Copyright 1993. International Chamber of Commerce / Chambre de Commerce Internationale

Advice for the Beneficiary

Commercial Invoice, one original and 3 copies

Multimodal Transport Document issued to the order of the French Importer Co.
marked freight prepaid and notify XYZ Custom House Broker Inc.

Insurance Certificate covering the Institute Cargo Clauses and the Institute War
and Strike Clauses for 110% of the invoice value endorsed to The French Importer Co.

Certificate of Origin evidencing goods to be of U.S.A. Origin

Packing List

Covering: Machinery and spare parts as per pro-forma invoice number 657
dated December 17, 1993 - CIP INCOTERMS 1990

Documents to be presented within [14] days after the date of shipment but within the validity of the Credit.

We hereby issue the Irrevocable Documentary Credit in your favour. It is subject to the Uniform Customs and Practice for Documentary Credits (1993 Revision, International Chamber of Commerce, Paris, France, Publication No. 500) and engages us in accordance with the terms thereof. The number and the date of the Credit and the name of our bank must be quoted on all drafts required. If the Credit is available by negotiation, each presentation must be noted on the reverse side of this advice by the bank where the Credit is available.

This document consists of [1] signed page(s)

The French Issuing Bank

2. *Irrevocable Negotiation Documentary Credit*

See page 40

Definition

Under the Irrevocable Negotiation Documentary Credit, the Issuing Bank's engagement is extended to third parties who negotiate or purchase the Beneficiary's Draft/documents presented under the Documentary Credit. This assures anyone who is authorised to negotiate Draft(s)/document(s) that these Drafts/documents will be duly honoured by the Issuing Bank provided the terms and conditions of the Documentary Credit are complied with. A bank which effectively negotiates Draft(s)/document(s) buys them from the Beneficiary, thereby becoming a holder in due course.

The engagement of the Issuing Bank is normally indicated in the Documentary Credit as available for negotiation by a Nominated Bank and expiring for presentation of documents at the offices of such a Nominated Bank. Alternatively, the engagement of the Issuing Bank may be stated more explicitly as follows:

"We hereby agree with the drawers, endorsers, and bona fide holders of Drafts/documents drawn under and in compliance with the terms and conditions of the Credit that such Drafts/documents will be duly honoured on due presentation if (negotiated) or (presented at this office) on or before (the expiry date)", or words of similar intent.

Irrevocable Negotiation Documentary Credit

Name of Issuing Bank: The French Issuing Bank 38 rue françois 1er 75008 Paris, France	**Irrevocable Documentary Credit**	Number 12345

Place and Date of Issue: Paris, 1 January 1994

Applicant: The French Importer Co. 89 rue du Commerce Paris, France	**Expiry Date and Place for Presentation of Documents** Expiry Date: May 29, 1994 Place for Presentation: The American Advising Bank, Tampa
	Beneficiary: The American Exporter Co. Inc. 17 Main Street Tampa, Florida
Advising Bank: Reference. No The American Advising Bank 456 Commerce Avenue Tampa, Florida	**Amount:** US$100,000.- one hundred thousand U.S.Dollars

Partial shipments [X] allowed [ ] not allowed	**Credit available with Nominated Bank:** The American Advising Bank
Transhipment [X] allowed [ ] not allowed	[ ] by payment at sight
	[ ] by deferred payment at:
[ ] Insurance covered by buyers	[ ] by acceptance of drafts at:
	[X] by negotiation
Shipment as defined in UCP 500 Article 46	Against the documents detailed herein:
From: Tampa, Florida	[ ] and Beneficiary's draft(s) drawn on:
For transportation to: Paris, France	
Not later than: May 15, 1994	The French Issuing Bank, Paris, France

Advice for the Beneficiary

Commercial Invoice, one original and 3 copies

Multimodal Transport Document issued to the order of the French Importer Co.
marked freight prepaid and notify XYZ Custom House Broker Inc.

Insurance Certificate covering the Institute Cargo Clauses and the Institute War
and Strike Clauses for 110% of the invoice value endorsed to The French Importer Co.

Certificate of Origin evidencing goods to be of U.S.A. Origin

Packing List

Covering: Machinery and spare parts as per pro-forma invoice number 657
dated December 17, 1993 - CIP INCOTERMS 1990

Documents to be presented within [14] days after the date of shipment but within the validity of the Credit.

We hereby issue the Irrevocable Documentary Credit in your favour. It is subject to the Uniform Customs and Practice for Documentary Credits (1993 Revision, International Chamber of Commerce, Paris, France, Publication No. 500) and engages us in accordance with the terms thereof. The number and the date of the Credit and the name of our bank must be quoted on all drafts required. If the Credit is available by negotiation, each presentation must be noted on the reverse side of this advice by the bank where the Credit is available.

This document consists of [1] signed page(s)

The French Issuing Bank

3. *Irrevocable Documentary Credit (Unconfirmed Documentary Credit)*

See pages 42–43

Definition

The Issuing Bank's irrevocable Documentary Credit is advised through an Advising Bank. The Advising Bank acts as agent of the Issuing Bank and does not assume any responsibility to the Beneficiary under the Documentary Credit except for taking reasonable care to check the apparent authenticity of the Documentary Credit which it advises.

The Advising Bank will inform the beneficiary that it is passing on the Issuing Bank's Documentary Credit and will add to this advice the following:

"This notification and the enclosed advice are sent to you without any engagement on our part", or words of similar intent.

Irrevocable Documentary Credit (Unconfirmed) Advice

Name of Advising Bank The American Advising Bank 456 Commerce Avenue Tampa, Florida	**Notification of Irrevocable Documentary Credit**
Reference Number of Advising Bank: 2417	
Place and date of Notification: January 14, 1994, Tampa	
Issuing Bank: The French Issuing Bank 38 rue François 1er Paris, France	**Beneficiary:** The American Exporter Co. Inc 17 Main Strret Tampa, Florida
Reference Number of the Issuing Bank: 12345	**Amount:** US$100,000.- One hundred thousand U.S. Dollars

We have been informed by the above-mentioned Issuing Bank that the above-mentioned Documentary Credit has been issued in your favour.
Please find enclosed the advice intended for you.

Check the Credit terms and conditions carefully. In the event you do not agree with the terms and conditions, or if you feel unable to comply with
any of those terms and conditions, kindly arrange an amendment of the Credit through your contracting party (the Applicant).

Other information:

[X]   This notification and the enclosed advice are sent to you without any engagement on our part.

[ ]   As requested by the Issuing Bank, we hereby add our confirmation to this Credit in accordance with the stipulations under UCP 500 Article 9.

The American Advising Bank

Irrevocable Documentary Credit (Unconfirmed)

Name of Issuing Bank: The French Issuing Bank 38 rue François 1er 75008 Paris, France	**Irrevocable Documentary Credit**	Number 12345

Place and Date of Issue: Paris, 1 January 1994

Expiry Date and Place for Presentation of Documents

Expiry Date: May 29, 1994

Place for Presentation: The American Advising Bank, Tampa

Applicant:

The French Importer Co.
89 rue du Commerce
Paris, France

Beneficiary:

The American Exporter Co. Inc.
17 Main Street
Tampa, Florida

Advising Bank: Reference. No

The American Advising Bank
456 Commerce Avenue
Tampa, Florida

Amount:

US$100,000.- one hundred thousand U.S.Dollars

Partial shipments [X] allowed [ ] not allowed

Transhipment [X] allowed [ ] not allowed

[ ] Insurance covered by buyers

Credit available with Nominated Bank: The American Advising Bank

[ ] by payment at sight

[ ] by deferred payment at:

[ ] by acceptance of drafts at:

[X] by negotiation

Shipment as defined in UCP 500 Article 46

From: Tampa, Florida

For transportation to: Paris, France

Not later than: May 15, 1994

Against the documents detailed herein:

[X] and Beneficiary's draft(s) drawn on:

The French Issuing Bank, Paris, France

Advice for the Beneficiary

Commercial Invoice, one original and 3 copies

Multimodal Transport Document issued to the order of the French Importer Co.
marked freight prepaid and notify XYZ Custom House Broker Inc.

Insurance Certificate covering the Institute Cargo Clauses and the Institute War
and Strike Clauses for 110% of the invoice value endorsed to The French Importer Co.

Certificate of Origin evidencing goods to be of U.S.A. Origin

Packing List

Covering: Machinery and spare parts as per pro-forma invoice number 657
dated December 17, 1993 - CIP INCOTERMS 1990

Documents to be presented within [14] days after the date of shipment but within the validity of the Credit.

We hereby issue the Irrevocable Documentary Credit in your favour. It is subject to the Uniform Customs and Practice for Documentary Credits (1993 Revision, International Chamber of Commerce, Paris, France, Publication No. 500) and engages us in accordance with the terms thereof. The number and the date of the Credit and the name of our bank must be quoted on all drafts required. If the Credit is available by negotiation, each presentation must be noted on the reverse side of this advice by the bank where the Credit is available.

This document consists of [1] signed page(s)

The French Issuing Bank

4. *Irrevocable Confirmed Documentary Credit*

See pages 46–47

Definition

A confirmation of an irrevocable Documentary Credit by a bank (the Confirming Bank) upon the authorisation or request of the Issuing Bank constitutes a definite undertaking of the Confirming Bank, in addition to that of the Issuing Bank, provided that the stipulated documents are presented to the Confirming Bank or to any other Nominated Bank on or before the expiry date and the terms and conditions of the Documentary Credit are complied with, to pay, to accept Draft(s) or to negotiate.

A double assurance of payment

An irrevocable Confirmed Documentary Credit gives the Beneficiary a double assurance of payment, since it represents both the undertaking of the Issuing Bank and the undertaking of the Confirming Bank. The second obligor (the Confirming Bank) engages that drawings under the Documentary Credit will be duly honoured in accordance with the terms and conditions of the Documentary Credit.

Normally, one considers the classification of the credit and the financial standing of the Issuing Bank. If an Issuing Bank is considered to be a first class bank, there may not be any need to have its Documentary Credit confirmed by another bank. Nevertheless, the Beneficiary may desire that the Documentary Credit and payment thereunder be guaranteed by a bank located in his own country. In such a situation, such Confirming Bank becomes legally liable to the Beneficiary to the same extent that the Issuing Bank does. Despite the fact that **UCP 500 Article 2** states "... For the purpose of these Articles, branches of a bank in different countries are considered another bank", the Beneficiary should review the confirmation of a Documentary Credit given by a branch or a subsidiary of the Issuing Bank to see whether it is indeed another separate and distinct bank obligation under the Documentary Credit.

Silent confirmation

Silent confirmation represents an agreement between a bank and the Beneficiary for that bank to "add its confirmation" to the Documentary Credit despite not being so authorised by the Issuing Bank.

The Beneficiary wishes to obtain the security of "the Confirming Bank" and is willing to pay the "confirmation commission" due, but the Beneficiary does not wish to request the Applicant to instruct the Issuing Bank to give its authorisation to have another bank confirm its Documentary Credit.

Under **UCP 500 sub-Article 9(b)**, the Documentary Credit may only be confirmed if it is so authorised or requested by the Issuing Bank. Therefore, the Documentary Credit may not be confirmed when it has not been authorised or requested by the Issuing Bank. Nevertheless, the fact that such an unauthorised "confirmation" may have been effected extends the responsibility of the bank which "confirmed" the Documentary Credit against the Beneficiary, without recourse as a "Confirming Bank" to the Issuing Bank which clearly did not request or authorise the bank to "add its confirmation". The "Confirming Bank" does not acquire the same rights to the Credit as the Issuing Bank and is not a "Confirming Bank" in any sense of the word. In effect, there has not been a "confirmation" but a separate arrangement between the Beneficiary and the "confirming bank" which "confirmed" the Documentary Credit under which said bank is irrevocably obligated, subject to compliance, to purchase or discount the Draft(s) and/or document(s) drawn and presented by the Beneficiary, and usually without recourse.

Irrevocable Confirmed Documentary Credit Advice

Name of Advising Bank The American Advising Bank 456 Commerce Avenue Tampa, Florida	**Notification of Irrevocable Documentary Credit**

Reference Number of Advising Bank: 2417	
Place and date of Notification: January 14, 1994, Tampa	

Issuing Bank: The French Issuing Bank 38 rue François 1er Paris, France	**Beneficiary:** The American Exporter Co. Inc 17 Main Street Tampa, Florida

Reference Number of the Issuing Bank: 12345	**Amount:** US$100,000.- One hundred thousand U.S. Dollars

We have been informed by the above-mentioned Issuing Bank that the above-mentioned Documentary Credit has been issued in your favour.
Please find enclosed the advice intended for you.

Check the Credit terms and conditions carefully. In the event you do not agree with the terms and conditions, or if you feel unable to comply with any of those terms and conditions, kindly arrange an amendment of the Credit through your contracting party (the Applicant).

Other information:

☐ This notification and the enclosed advice are sent to you without any engagement on our part.

☒ As requested by the Issuing Bank, we hereby add our confirmation to this Credit in accordance with the stipulations under UCP 500 Article 9.

The American Advising Bank

Irrevocable Confirmed Documentary Credit

Name of Issuing Bank: The French Issuing Bank 38 rue François 1er 75008 Paris, France	**Irrevocable Documentary Credit** Number 12345

Place and Date of Issue: Paris, 1 January 1994

Applicant: The French Importer Co. 89 rue du Commerce Paris, France	**Expiry Date and Place for Presentation of Documents** Expiry Date: May 29, 1994 Place for Presentation: The American Advising Bank, Tampa
Advising Bank: Reference. No The American Advising Bank 456 Commerce Avenue Tampa, Florida	**Beneficiary:** The American Exporter Co. Inc. 17 Main Street Tampa, Florida
	Amount: US$100,000.- one hundred thousand U.S.Dollars

Partial shipments [X] allowed [ ] not allowed

Transhipment [X] allowed [ ] not allowed

[ ] Insurance covered by buyers

Credit available with Nominated Bank: The American Advising Bank, Tampa

[X] by payment at sight

[ ] by deferred payment at:

[ ] by acceptance of drafts at:

[ ] by negotiation

Shipment as defined in UCP 500 Article 46

From: Tampa, Florida

For transportation to: Paris, France

Not later than: May 15, 1994

Against the documents detailed herein:

[X] and Beneficiary's draft(s) drawn on: The American Advising Bank

Advice for the Beneficiary

Commercial Invoice, one original and 3 copies

Multimodal Transport Document issued to the order of the French Importer Co.
marked freight prepaid and notify XYZ Custom House Broker Inc

Insurance Certificate covering the Institute Cargo Clauses and the Institute War
and Strike Clauses for 110% of the invoice value endorsed to The French Importer Co.

Certificate of Origin evidence goods to be of U.S.A. Origin

Packing List

Covering: Machinerie and spare parts as per pro-forma invoice number 657
dated December 17, 1993 - CIP INCOTERMS 1990

Documents to be presented within [14] days after the date of shipment but within the validity of the Credit.

We hereby issue the Irrevocable Documentary Credit in your favour. It is subject to the Uniform Customs and Practice for Documentary Credits (1993 Revision, International Chamber of Commerce, Paris, France, Publication No. 500) and engages us in accordance with the terms thereof. The number and the date of the Credit and the name of our bank must be quoted on all drafts required. If the Credit is available by negotiation, each presentation must be noted on the reverse side of this advice by the bank where the Credit is available.

This document consists of [1] signed page(s)   The French Issuing Bank

5. *Revolving Documentary Credit*

☞ Definition

A Revolving Documentary Credit is one by which, under the terms and conditions thereof, the amount is renewed or reinstated without specific amendments to the Documentary Credit being required. The Revolving Documentary Credit may be revocable or irrevocable, and may revolve in relation to time or value.

In the case of a Documentary Credit that revolves in relation to time, e.g. which is initially available for up to $15,000 per month during a fixed period of time, say, six months, the Documentary Credit is automatically available for $15,000 each month irrespective of whether any sum was drawn during the previous month. A Documentary Credit of this nature can be cumulative or non-cumulative. If it is stated to be "cumulative", any sum not utilised during the first period carries over and may be utilised during a subsequent period. If it is "non-cumulative", any sum not utilised in a period ceases to be available, that is, it is not carried over to a subsequent period. It must be remembered that under this kind of Documentary Credit and following this example, the obligations of the Issuing Bank would be for $90,000, i.e. six revolving periods each for $15,000, so while the face value of the Documentary Credit is given as $15,000 the total undertaking of the Issuing Bank is for the full value that might be drawn.

In the case of a Documentary Credit that revolves in relation to value, the amount is reinstated upon utilisation within a given overall period of validity. The Documentary Credit may provide for automatic reinstatement immediately upon presentation of the specified documents, or it may provide for reinstatement only after receipt by the Issuing Bank of those documents or another stated condition. This kind of Documentary Credit involves the buyer and the banks in an incalculable liability. For that reason, it is not in common use. To maintain a degree of control, it would be necessary to specify the overall amount that may be drawn under the Documentary Credit. Such amount would have to be decided by the buyer and the seller to meet their requirements, and would have to be agreed to by the Issuing Bank.

6. *Red Clause Documentary Credit*

☞ **Definition**

A Red Clause Documentary Credit is a Documentary Credit with a special condition incorporated into it that authorises the Confirming Bank or any other Nominated Bank to make advances to the Beneficiary before presentation of the documents.

The clause is incorporated at the specific request of the Applicant, and the wording is dependent upon his requirements. The Red Clause Documentary Credit is so called because the clause was originally written in red ink to draw attention to the unique nature of this Documentary Credit. The clause specifies the amount of the advance authorised, which, in some instances, may be for the full amount of the Documentary Credit.

The Red Clause Documentary Credit is often used as a method of providing the seller with funds prior to shipment. Therefore, it is of value to middlemen and dealers in areas of commerce that require a form of pre-financing and when a buyer would be willing to make special concessions of this nature.

For example, it could be used by a wool importer in England to enable a wool shipper in Australia to obtain funds to pay the actual suppliers (either by direct purchase or through the wool auctions) by obtaining a loan from the Australian bank, either on an unsecured basis or against the security of interim documents. This would enable repayment of the loan, plus interest, from the proceeds due to the Australian Beneficiary when the wool was shipped and documents were presented in accordance with the terms of the Documentary Credit. If, however, the Beneficiary failed to ship the wool so as to repay the loan by presenting documents called for by the Documentary Credit, the Australian bank would have the right to demand repayment, with interest, from the Issuing Bank and that bank would have a similar right of recourse against the Applicant.

This kind of arrangement places the onus of final repayment on the Applicant, who would be liable for repayment of the advances if the Beneficiary failed to present the documents called for under the Documentary Credit, and who would also be liable for all costs - such as interest or foreign exchange hedging - incurred by the Issuing Bank, the Confirming Bank, if any or any other Nominated Bank.

7. *Standby Credits*

☞ Definition

The Standby Credit is a Documentary Credit or similar arrangement, however named or described, which represents an obligation to the Beneficiary on the part of the Issuing Bank to:

(1)   repay money borrowed by the Applicant, or advanced to or for the account of the Applicant;

(2)   make payment on account of any indebtedness undertaken by the Applicant; or

(3)   make payment on account of any default by the Applicant in the performance of an obligation.

The Standby Credit thus serves as a back-up or secondary means of payment, though it is recognised as a primary obligation of the Issuing Bank. In both types of usage, Commercial or Standby Documentary Credits alike, the underlying purpose of the Issuing Bank is to pay for goods supplied or services furnished, as required by the contract between the parties.
The difference in application can be expressed by saying that the Commercial Documentary Credit is activated by the "performance" of the Beneficiary.
The Standby Credit, by contrast, supports the Beneficiary in the event of a "default".

8. *Transferable Documentary Credit*

There are two methods allowing for transferring the Beneficiary's rights to a
third party: assignment and transfer. The difference is that under an
assignment the Beneficiary assigns or transfers to a third party his rights to the
proceeds to which he may be, or may become, entitled under a Documentary
Credit, in accordance with the provisions of the applicable law. Under the
transfer the Beneficiary assigns or transfers his right to perform under the
Documentary Credit to a third party (the Second Beneficiary(ies)).

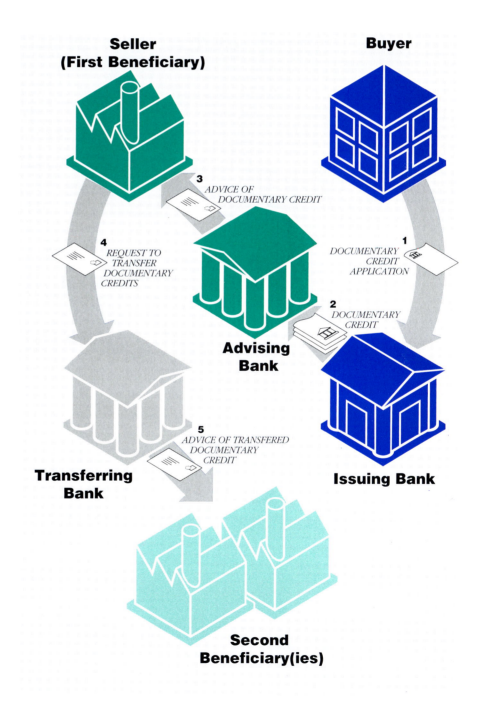

☞ ### Definition

A Transferable Documentary Credit is a Credit under which the Beneficiary (First Beneficiary) may request the bank authorised to pay, incur a deferred payment undertaking, accept or negotiate (the "Transferring Bank"), or in the event of a freely negotiable Credit, the bank specifically authorised in the Credit as a Transferring Bank to make the Documentary Credit available in whole or in part to one or more other Beneficiary(ies) (Second Beneficiary(ies)).

It should be recognised, however, that despite the requirement for a specific authorisation for transfer in the Documentary Credit, as stated in **UCP 500 sub-Article 48(b)**, there may be occasions, under the respective laws of the country, where a Documentary Credit may be transferred even though it is not authorised by the Documentary Credit: for instance, when the Beneficiary has gone into bankruptcy or insolvency, when there are liquidators of the company, when there are corporate reorganisations, etc.

Advantages and disadvantages

- The transferee obtains the right to make presentation of Drafts and documents and to make demand for payment, and
- the buyer accepts the risk of receiving goods from a third party who may not be known to him and with whom he has had no business dealings.

First Beneficiary's instructions and amendments

In accordance with **UCP 500 sub-Article 48(d)**, the Beneficiary must, at the time of making a request for transfer and prior to the transfer of the Documentary Credit, irrevocably instruct the Transferring Bank whether or not he retains the right to refuse to allow the Transferring Bank to advise amendments to the Second Beneficiary(ies). Furthermore, both the Applicant and the Beneficiary should understand that in accordance with **UCP 500 sub-Article 48(e)**, if a Documentary Credit is transferred to more than one Second Beneficiary(ies), refusal of an amendment by one or more Second Beneficiary(ies) does not invalidate the acceptance(s) by the other Second Beneficiary(ies) with respect to whom the Documentary Credit will be amended accordingly. With respect to the Second Beneficiary(ies) who rejected the amendment, the Documentary Credit will remain unamended.

Recommended forms for requesting a transfer of the Credit

The following suggested forms are offered in an attempt to guide the parties under a transferable Documentary Credit. They are solely for guidance and there should be no legal imputation attached to them.

Request for a full transfer of the Documentary Credit
with retainment of rights on amendments

```
Domicile and Date of Request:

To:            The Transferring Bank
               Street Address or P.O. Box
               City, and Country

Reference:     Issuing Bank's Documentary Credit Number
               Advising Bank's Reference Number

Suggested text:
The undersigned Beneficiary hereby irrevocably transfers to:
(Name and complete address of the Transferee)
all rights of the undersigned Beneficiary in such Documentary
Credit, to draw up to but not exceeding a sum of (amount).

The Transferee shall have the sole rights as Beneficiary thereof,
provided that this transfer expires on (expiry date of the
transfer but not later than the expiry date of the Credit).

In accordance with UCP 500 sub-Article 48 (d), the undersigned
Beneficiary retains the right to refuse to allow the Transferring
Bank to advise amendments made under the original Documentary
Credit to the Transferee. Therefore, the Transferring Bank must
obtain approval of the undersigned Beneficiary before advising
amendments to the Transferee.

If you agree to these instructions, please advise the Transferee
the terms and conditions of the transferred Credit and these
instructions.

Signature of the Beneficiary
Authentication of the Beneficiary's signature by a bank
```

Request for a full transfer of the Documentary Credit
with partial waiver of rights on amendments

```
Domicile and Date of Request:

To:            The Transferring Bank
               Street Address or P.O. Box
               City, and Country

Reference:     Issuing Bank's Documentary Credit Number
               Advising Bank's Reference Number

Suggested text:
The undersigned Beneficiary hereby irrevocably transfers to:
(Name and complete address of the Transferee) all rights of the
undersigned Beneficiary in such Documentary Credit, to draw up to
but not exceeding a sum of (amount).

The Transferee shall have the sole rights as Beneficiary thereof,
provided that this transfer expires on (expiry date of the
transfer but not later than the expiry date of the Credit).

In accordance with UCP 500 sub-Article 48 (d), the undersigned
Beneficiary waives his right (except an indicated below) to
refuse to allow the Transferring Bank to advise amendments made
under the original Documentary Credit to the Transferee.
Therefore, the Transferee shall have the sole rights as
Beneficiary including sole rights relating to any amendments to
the Documentary Credit whether now existing or hereafter made,
provided however, that this transfer of the Documentary Credit
shall not give to the Transferee rights in any amendments
hereafter made (1) increasing the amount, and/or (2) extending
the expiration date of the Documentary Credit. (Indicate whether
one or both conditions apply).

Amendments relating to (1) increases, and/or (2) extensions
(Indicate whether one or both conditions apply) are to be advised
to the Transferee only with the consent of the undersigned
Beneficiary.  All other amendments are to be advised directly to
the Transferee.
If you agree to these instructions, please advise the Transferee
the terms and conditions of the transferred Credit and these
instructions.

Signature of the Beneficiary
Authentication of the Beneficiary's signature by a bank
```

Request for a full transfer of the Documentary Credit with waiver of rights on amendments

Domicile and Date of Request:

To: The Transferring Bank
Street Address or P.O. Box
City, and Country

Reference: Issuing Bank's Documentary Credit Number
Advising Bank's Reference Number

Suggested text:
The undersigned Beneficiary hereby irrevocably transfers to:
(Name and complete address of the Transferee) all rights of the
undersigned Beneficiary in such Documentary Credit, to draw up to
but not exceeding a sum of (amount).

The Transferee shall have the sole rights as Beneficiary thereof,
provided that this transfer expires on (expiry date of the
transfer but not later than the expiry date of the Credit).

In accordance with UCP 500 sub-Article 48 (d), the undersigned
Beneficiary waives his right to refuse to allow the Transferring
Bank to advise amendments made under the original Documentary
Credit to the Transferee. Therefore, the Transferee shall have
the sole rights as Beneficiary including sole rights relating to
any amendments to the Documentary Credit whether increases or
extensions or other amendments and whether now existing or
hereafter made. All amendments are to be advised directly to the
Transferee.

If you agree to these instructions, please advise the Transferee
the terms and conditions of the transferred Credit and these
instructions.

Signature of the Beneficiary
Authentication of the Beneficiary's signature by a bank

Request for a partial transfer of the Documentary Credit with retainment of rights on amendments

```
Domicile and Date of Request:

To:              The Transferring Bank
                 Street Address or P.O. Box
                 City, and Country

Reference:       Issuing Bank's Documentary Credit Number
                 Advising Bank's Reference Number

Suggested text:
The undersigned Beneficiary hereby irrevocably transfers a
partial interest of the undersigned Beneficiary in such
Documentary Credit to: (Name and complete address of the
Transferee) to draw up to but not exceeding a sum of (amount)
under the above Documentary Credit; provided that this transfer
expires on (expiry date of the transfer but not later than the
expiry date of the Credit).

In accordance with UCP 500 sub-Article 48 (d), the undersigned
Beneficiary retains the right to refuse to allow the Transferring
Bank to advise amendments made under the original Documentary
Credit to the Transferee.  Therefore, the Transferring Bank must
obtain approval of the undersigned Beneficiary before advising
amendments to the Transferee.

If you agree to these instructions, please advise the Transferee
the terms and conditions of the transferred Credit and these
instructions.

Signature of the Beneficiary
Authentication of the Beneficiary's signature by a bank
```

Request for a partial transfer of the Documentary Credit with partial waiver of rights on amendments

Domicile and Date of Request:

To: The Transferring Bank
Street Address or P.O. Box
City, and Country

Reference: Issuing Bank's Documentary Credit Number
Advising Bank's Reference Number

Suggested text:
The undersigned Beneficiary hereby irrevocably transfers to:
(Name and complete address of the Transferee) all rights of the
undersigned Beneficiary in such Documentary Credit, to draw up to
but not exceeding a sum of (amount).

The Transferee shall have the sole rights as Beneficiary thereof,
provided that this transfer expires on (expiry date of the
transfer but not later than the expiry date of the Credit).

In accordance with UCP 500 sub-Article 48 (d), the undersigned
Beneficiary waives his right (except an indicated below) to
refuse to allow the Transferring Bank to advise amendments made
under the original Documentary Credit to the Transferee.
Therefore, the Transferee shall have the sole rights as
Beneficiary including sole rights relating to any amendments to
the Documentary Credit whether now existing or hereafter made,
provided however, that this transfer of the Documentary Credit
shall not give to the Transferee rights in any amendments
hereafter made (1) increasing the amount, and/or (2) extending
the expiration date of the Documentary Credit (Indicate whether
one or both conditions apply).

Amendments relating to (1) increases, and/or (2) extensions
(Indicate whether one or both conditions apply) are to be advised
to the Transferee only with the consent of the undersigned
Beneficiary. All other amendments are to be advised directly to
the Transferee.

If you agree to these instructions, please advise the Transferee
the terms and conditions of the transferred Credit and these
instructions.

Signature of the Beneficiary
Authentication of the Beneficiary's signature by a bank

Request for a partial transfer of the Documentary Credit with retainment of rights on amendments and substitution of invoice privilege

Domicile and Date of Request:

To: The Transferring Bank
             Street Address or P.O. Box
             City, and Country

Reference: Issuing Bank's Documentary Credit Number
             Advising Bank's Reference Number

Suggested text:
The undersigned Beneficiary hereby irrevocably transfers a
partial interest of the undersigned Beneficiary in such
Documentary Credit to: (Name and complete address of the
Transferee) to draw under the above Documentary Credit subject to
the same terms and conditions with the exception of the
following:
          (a) Amount,
          (b) Quantity of Goods,
          (c) Unit price, if any,
          (d) Expiry date,
          (e) Last date for presentation of documents in accordance
               with UCP 500 Article 43,
          (f) The period for shipment,
          (g) The percentage of insurance cover,
          (h) Name of the Beneficiary to be substituted for that of the
               Applicant
          (indicate which of the above is applicable).

In accordance with UCP 500 sub-Article 48 (d), the undersigned
Beneficiary retains the right to refuse to allow the Transferring
Bank to advise amendments made under the original Documentary Credit
to the Transferee. Therefore, the Transferring Bank must obtain
approval of the undersigned Beneficiary before advising amendments to
the Transferee.

In accordance with UCP 500 sub-Article 48 (i), the undersigned
Beneficiary retains the right to substitute his own invoice(s) and
Draft(s) for those of the Transferee, for amounts not in excess of
the original amount stipulated in the Credit and for the original
unit prices if stipulated in the Credit, and upon such substitution
of invoice(s) (and Draft(s)), the undersigned Beneficiary can draw
under the Credit for the difference, if any, between such invoice(s)
and the Transferee's invoice(s).

It is understood that in the event the undersigned Beneficiary fails
to supply his own invoice(s) and Draft(s) in exchange for the
Transferee's invoice(s) (and Draft(s)) on first demand, the
Transferring Bank has the right to deliver to the Issuing Bank the
documents received under the transferred Credit, including the
Transferee's invoice(s) (and Draft(s)), without further
responsibility to the undersigned Beneficiary.

If you agree to these instructions, please advise the Transferee the
terms and conditions of the transferred Credit and these
instructions.

Signature of the Beneficiary

9. Assignment of Proceeds

In accordance with UCP 500 Article 49, the fact that a Documentary Credit is not stated to be transferable shall not affect the Beneficiary's right to assign any proceeds to which he may be, or may become, entitled under such Documentary Credit in accordance with the applicable law. This provision relates only to the assignment of proceeds and not to the assignment of the right to perform under the Documentary Credit itself.

1.

Beneficiary presents his documents to the Nominated Bank

2.

Paying/Negotiating Bank remits to the Beneficiary any funds not assigned

3.

Paying/Negotiating Bank remits to the Assignee the funds assigned due to him

4.

Paying/Negotiating Bank remits the documents to the Issuing Bank

5.

Issuing Bank reimburses the Paying/Negotiating Bank in accordance with their arrangement

6.

Issuing Bank remits the documents to the Applicant

7.

Applicant reimburses the Issuing Bank in accordance with their arrangement

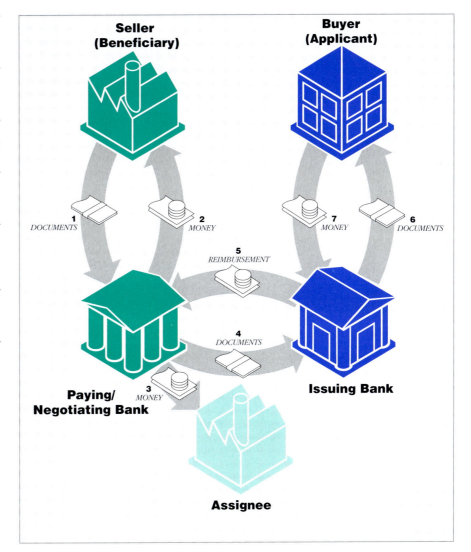

Mechanics of assignment

Under an assignment of proceeds request, the parties must ask the following questions:

- What is being assigned?
- On which terms is the Documentary Credit available?
  - at sight?
  - by acceptance?
  - by deferred payment?

How to control an effective assignment of proceeds

- Written notification by the Beneficiary to the Nominated Bank, giving his instructions for the assignment of the proceeds must be irrevocable and in writing, which instructions obligate the Beneficiary himself vis-a-vis the Nominated Bank to present the required Drafts and/or documents under the Documentary Credit and that payment, if and when effected, is to be made in accordance with those instructions,

- The Beneficiary's instructions should be manually signed and bear a bank's (or another institution's) guarantee which confirms the authenticity and the authority of the signer of that document,

- The Nominated Bank, if it agrees to such instructions, must acknowledge and notify the assignee of the instructions lodged and the Nominated Bank's agreement to perform in accordance therewith,

- The Nominated Bank which is authorised to negotiate or pay should bear in mind that, if it decides to pay or negotiate the Drafts and/or documents drawn under the Documentary Credit, it must disburse the funds as instructed,

- If an Advising Bank or another Nominated Bank (not the Issuing Bank or the Confirming Bank) is instructed by the Beneficiary to accept such assignment of proceeds instructions, such bank is not obligated under the Documentary Credit to accept such instructions. However, if such Advising Bank or Nominated Bank does accept such instructions for assignment of proceeds, such bank should not mislead the assignee into believing that he has that bank's irrevocable obligation to pay as a result of those instructions. The statement to the assignee from such a bank should be phrased in such a manner that the assignee is aware of that bank's limited undertaking.

10. *Back-to-Back Documentary Credit*

It may happen that the Documentary Credit in favour of the Beneficiary is not transferable, or, although transferable, cannot meet the commercial requirements of transfer in accordance with **UCP 500 Article 48** conditions. The Beneficiary himself, however, may be unable to supply the goods and may need to purchase them from and make payment to another supplier. In this case, it may sometimes be possible to use a Back-to-Back Documentary Credit.

1.

Applicant instructs Issuing Bank to issue an irrevocable Credit in favour of the Beneficiary

2.

Issuing Bank issues the Credit and forwards it to the Beneficiary through the Advising Bank

3.

The Advising Bank advises the Credit to the Beneficiary

4.

The Beneficiary submits his original Credit to support a Second Credit to be issued by a bank in favour of the Second Beneficiary

5.

The second Issuing Bank issues the Back-to-Back Credit in favour of the new Beneficiary and forwards it through the Second Advising Bank

6.

The Second Advising Bank advises the Credit to the new Beneficiary

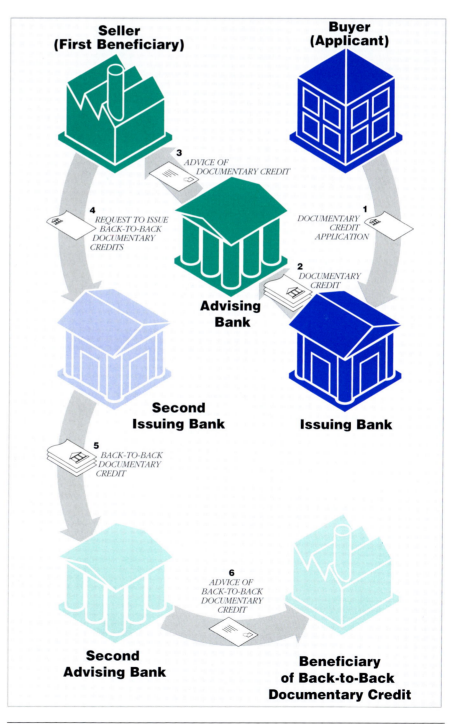

☞ **Definition**

The benefit of an irrevocable Documentary Credit (the Primary Credit) may be made available to a third party where the Primary Beneficiary uses the Documentary Credit as security/collateral to obtain another Documentary Credit (the Secondary Credit) in favour of the actual supplier.

This type of Documentary Credit is essential when the terms and conditions of a transferable Documentary Credit cannot be applied to the transaction.

A Back-to-Back Documentary Credit involves two separate Documentary Credits:

■ one opened in favour of the First or Primary Beneficiary, and

■ one opened for the account of the First/Primary Beneficiary in favour of a Second Beneficiary who is supplying the goods. The First/Primary Beneficiary of the first Documentary Credit becomes the Applicant for the second Documentary Credit. Under this arrangement, the Beneficiary of the Secondary Credit obtains greater protection than he would under an assignment of proceeds.

With the Back-to-Back Documentary Credit, the Secondary Credit should be worded so as to produce the documents (apart from the commercial invoice) required by the Primary Credit, and to produce them within the time limits set by the Primary Credit, in order that the Primary Beneficiary under the Primary Credit may be able to present his documents within the limits of the Primary Credit.

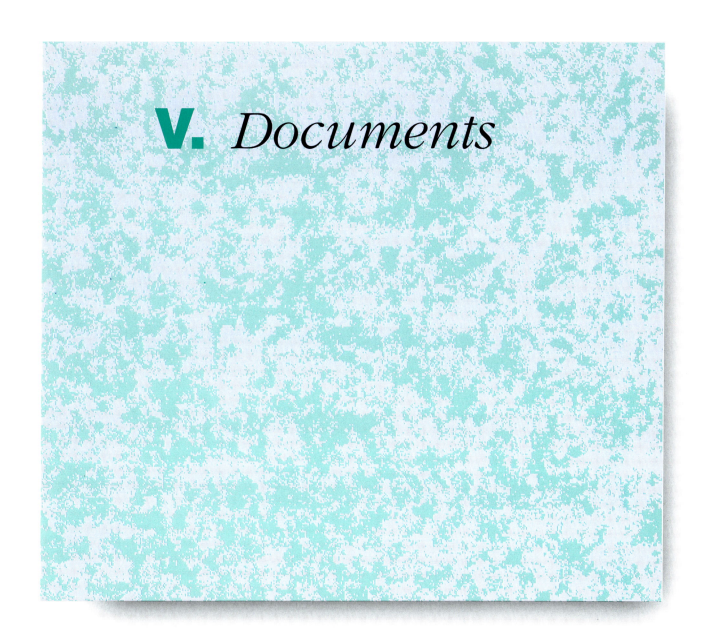

V. Documents

1. Draft (Bill of Exchange)

☞ ## Definition

A bill of exchange is an unconditional order in writing, addressed by one person to another, signed by the person giving it, requiring the person to whom it is addressed to pay on demand or at a fixed or determinable future time a sum certain in money to or to the order of a specified person, or to bearer.

Specimen of a draft

Exchange for US$100,000.-	Tampa, May 27, 1994

At sight of the bill of exchange pay to the order of ourselves
One hundred thousand and 00/000 US dollars

Drawn under The French Issuing Bank, Paris, France Documentary Credit No. 12345

Value received and charge same to account of

TO: The French Issuing Bank
        38 rue François 1er
        75008, Paris, France

The American Exporter Co. Inc

UNCITRAL bill of exchange format

Tampa, May 27 1994
US$100,000

At sixty days after sight for values received,

pay against this bill of exchange to the

order of ourselves

the sum of US dollars one

hundred thousand

effective payment to be made in US dollars

only without deduction for and free of any

tax, import levy or duty

present or future of any nature under the

laws of the United States or any political

subdivision thereof or therein.

This bill of exchange is
payable at
The American Bank in Tampa

Drawn on The American
Advising Bank, Tampa

Accepted ....

For and on behalf of
The American Exporter Co. Inc.
Tampa, Florida

2. Commercial Invoice UCP 500 Article 37

☞ Definition

A commercial invoice is the accounting document by which the seller claims payment from the buyer for the value of the goods and/or services being supplied.

Specimen of an invoice

A commercial invoice normally includes the following information:

- name and address of the seller,

- date of issue,

- invoice number,

- name and address of the buyer,

- order or contract number, quantity and description of the goods, unit price (and details of any other agreed charges not included in the unit price), and the total invoice price,

- shipping marks and numbers,

- terms of delivery and payment,

- shipping details, and

- any other information required by the Documentary Credit

INVOICE	FACTURE FACTURA	RECHNUNG FACTUUR

SELLER Name, Address, VAT No		Sheet No.
The American Exporter Co. Inc. 17 Main Street Tampa, Florida	**Invoice No. & Date (Tax Point)** 19 May 27, 1994	**Seller's Reference** 657
	Buyer's References	**Other References**

Consignee	Buyer (if not Consignee)
The French Importer Co. 89 rue du Commerce Paris, France	

	Country of Origin of Goods U.S.A.	Country of Destination France
	Terms of Delivery and Payment	

Vessel/Aircraft etc. Fawn	Port of Loading Tampa	CIP INCOTERMS 1990
Port of Discharge Le Havre		

Marks and Numbers and Container No.	Number and Kind of Packages Description of Goods	TT Code No.	TT Gross Wt (Kg)	Total Cube (m³)
1/24 U.S.A.	Machinery and spare parts as per pro-forma invoice number 657 dated December 17, 1993 CIP Incoterms 1990		3900	

Item/ pkges	Gross/Net/Cube	Description	Quantity	Unit Price	Selling Price
24		Machinery and spare parts as per pro-forma invoice number 657 dated December 17, 1993 CIP Incoterms 1990			US$100,000
				Invoice Total	US$100,000

The American Exporter Co. Inc.
17 Main Street
Tampa, Florida

Name of signatory

Place and Date of Issue

Signature

3. Certificate of Origin

It is recommended that the reader reviews **UCP 500 Articles 20 and 21** concerning the ambiguity which can arise concerning issuers of documents and unspecified issuers or contents of documents.

A certificate of origin is a statement signed by the appropriate authority, as required by the Documentary Credit, providing evidence of the origin of the goods.

In many countries a certificate of origin, although prepared by the exporter or his agent, has to be issued in a mandatory form and manner, with a certification by an independent organisation, e.g. a Chamber of Commerce.

The certificate of origin contains details of the shipment to which it relates, states the origin of the goods, and bears the signature, or the stamp or the seal of the certifying entity.

Unless the Documentary Credit stipulates otherwise, the certificate of origin will be accepted under a Documentary Credit as tendered provided it meets the requirements of the Documentary Credit and it is not inconsistent with the other documents. (See **UCP 500 sub-Article 13(a)**).

Specimen of a certificate of origin

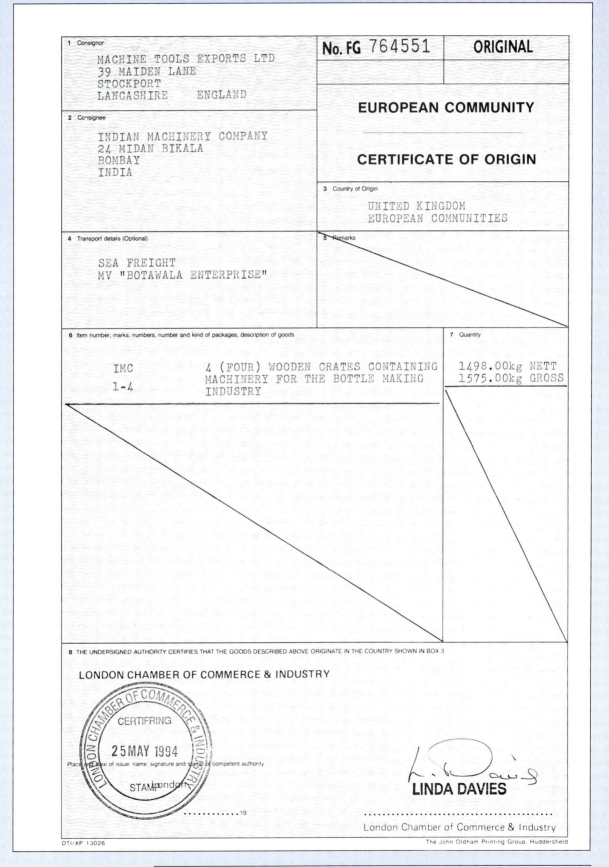

4. Insurance Document

The insurance document must:

1. be the one specified in the Documentary Credit (See **UCP 500 Article 34**),

2. cover the risks specified in the Documentary Credit (See **UCP 500 Article 35**),

3. be consistent with the other documents in its identification of the voyage and description of the goods. (See **UCP 500 sub-Articles 13(a) and 37(c)**).

4. unless otherwise stipulated in the Documentary Credit:

■ be a document issued and signed by insurance companies or underwriters or their agents, and must be presented in the full set of originals, if issued in more than one original,

■ indicate cover is effective at the latest from the date of loading on board or dispatch or taking in charge of the goods. (See **UCP 500 Article 34(e)**),

■ be for the CIF (cost, insurance and freight named port of destination, or CIP (freight/carriage and insurance paid to named place of destination) value of the goods, as the case may be, plus ten percent, but only when the CIF or CIP value can be determined from the documents on their face. Otherwise, the insurance coverage must be for a minimum of 110 percent of the amount for which payment, acceptance or negotiation is requested under the Documentary Credit, or 110 percent of the gross amount of the invoice, whichever is the greater. (See **UCP 500 sub-Article 33(f)**).

Specimen of an insurance document

Exporter	CERTIFICATE OF INSURANCE	
DERRCO ENGINEERING LTD 26 BELLOWS ROAD SITTINGBOURNE KENT		

Ins. Cert. No: L/A	90006	Exporters Ref:	55034/94
Code No. 66/AA/	499	Agents Ref:	EXC/19341

This is to certify that

ARTHENO FREIGHT SERVICES LTD

have been issued with an Open Policy and this certificate conveys all rights of the policy (for the purpose of collecting any loss or claim) as fully as if the property were covered by a special policy direct to the holder of this certificate but if the destination of the goods is outside the United Kingdom this certificate may require to be stamped within a given period in order to comply with the laws of the country of destination. Notwithstanding the description of the voyage stated herein, provided the goods are at the risk of the Assured this insurance shall attach from the time of leaving the warehouse, premises or place of storage in the interior.

MARITIME

INSURANCE COMPANY LIMITED

NORWICH UNION HOUSE,
51/54 FENCHURCH STREET, LONDON EC3M 3LA

Conveyance 'AMCO TRADER'	Port of Loading FELIXSTOWE	Insured Value (State Currency)
Port of Discharge NEW YORK	Final Destination ALBANY	£92,800 STERLING so valued

Marks, Nos./Container No.	No. and Kind of Packages	Description of Goods

IMPORTANT
PROCEDURE IN THE EVENT OF LOSS OR DAMAGE FOR WHICH UNDERWRITERS MAY BE LIABLE

LIABILITY OF CARRIERS, BAILEES OR OTHER THIRD PARTIES
It is the duty of the Assured and their Agents, in all cases, to take such measures as may be reasonable for the purpose of averting or minimising a loss and to ensure that all rights against Carriers, Bailees or other third parties are properly preserved and exercised. In particular, the Assured or their Agents are required:-
1 To claim immediately on the Carriers, Port Authorities or other Bailees for any missing packages.
2 In no circumstances except under written protest, to give clean receipts where goods are in doubtful condition.
3 When delivery is made by Container, to ensure that the Container and its seals are examined immediately by their responsible official.

If the Container is delivered damaged or with seals broken or missing or with seals other than as stated in the shipping documents, to clause the delivery receipt accordingly and retain all defective or irregular seals for subsequent identification.
4 To apply immediately for survey by Carriers' or other Bailees' Representatives if any loss or damage be apparent and claim on the Carriers or other Bailees for any actual loss or damage found at such survey.
5 To give notice in writing to the Carriers or other Bailees within three days of delivery if the loss or damage was not apparent at the time of taking delivery.
NOTE:- The Consignees or their Agents are recommended to make themselves familiar with the regulations of the Port Authorities at the port of discharge.

SURVEY AND CLAIM SETTLEMENT
In the event of loss or damage which may involve a claim under this insurance, immediate notice of such loss or damage should be given to and a Survey Report obtained from the Office or Agent nominated herein.
In the event of any claim arising under this insurance, request for settlement should be made to the Office or Agent nominated herein.
DOCUMENTATION OF CLAIMS
To enable claims to be dealt with promptly, the Assured or their Agents are advised to submit all available supporting documents without delay, including when applicable:-
1 Original policy or certificate of insurance.
2 Original or copy shipping invoices, together with shipping specification and/or weight notes.
3 Original Bill of Lading and/or other contract of carriage.
4 Survey report or other documentary evidence to show the extent of the loss or damage.
5 Landing account and weight notes at final destination.
6 Correspondence exchanged with the Carriers and other Parties regarding their liability for the loss or damage.

B. A. LANZARIO
2624 WESTFIELD AVENUE
ALBANY
NEW YORK
U.S.A.

    1 X 20' CONTAINER
    STC 160 CARTONS
    WEIGHING MACHINES

    FULL LOAD DOOR TO DOOR

    CONTAINER NO. UFCU. 221249/4

CONDITIONS
Subject to the current Institute Cargo Clauses (A) and/or AIR (as applicable). Subject to Institute Replacement Clause (as applicable). Subject to the Institute Radioactive Contamination Exclusion Clause CL.356 1.10.90.
Notwithstanding anything to the contary contained herein this insurance covers War and Strikes Risks in accordance with the current Institute War and Strikes Clauses which are deemed to be attached to and to form part of this certificate.
SURVEY CLAUSE
In the event of loss or damage which may give rise to a claim under this certificate, notice must be given immediately to the undernoted agent/s so that he/they may appoint a Surveyor if he/they so desire.

Agents at   NEW YORK   are OCEAN-AIR CARGO CLAIMS INC
     111 JOHN STREET, SUITE 1500, NEW YORK, NY 10038

CLAIMS
In the event of a claim arising under this Certificate it is agreed that it shall be settled in accordance with English Law and Custom and shall be so settled in
London or at   NEW YORK
                AS ABOVE

by

N. T. Ventker
Managing Director

This certificate is not valid unless countersigned

For	ARTHENO FREIGHT SERVICES LTD
Dated	10 JANUARY 1994
Signed	

MARD64–159–Jan 94   The original certificate must be produced when claim is made and must be surrendered on payment

5. Inspection Certificate

It is recommended that the reader reviews **UCP 500 Articles 20 and 21** concerning the ambiguity which can arise issuers of documents and unspecified issuers or contents of documents.

☞ **Definition**

An inspection certificate is a statement issued and signed by the appropriate authority, either a governmental entity or a private inspection company, providing evidence that the goods were inspected and detailing the results of such inspection.

In many countries, an inspection certificate is issued by an independent inspection company contracted for either by the buyer or by the seller, as stipulated in the Credit. For certain commodities or for certain countries, such an inspection certificate must be issued by a governmental entity.

The inspection certificate contains details of the shipment to which it relates, states the results of the inspection, and bears the signature, the stamp or the seal of the inspecting entity.

Unless the Documentary Credit stipulates otherwise, the inspection certificate will be accepted under a Documentary Credit tendered provided it meets the requirements of the Documentary Credit and it is not inconsistent with the other documents. (See **UCP 500 sub-Article 13(a)**).

Specimen of an inspection certificate

BUREAU VERITAS

CERTIFICAT	INSPECTION	Page 1 / 1
D'INSPECTION	CERTIFICATE	Code N. 0135736
		Date Paris, 17/09/1993
		BV n° XCI 9931245

CERTIFICATE OF INSPECTION

BUREAU VERITAS - Siège Social / Head Office - 17 bis, Place des Reflets - La Défense 2 - 92400 COURBEVOIE
Branche Produits et Commerce International / Commodities and International Trade Branch - Tél. 33 (1) 42 91 52 91 - Télex 612350 AGRI F

"Droits de reproduction strictement réservés (loi du 11 mars 1957). Toute imitation, reproduction non autorisée ou falsification du présent certificat constitue un faux en écritures privées, délit prévu et réprimé par les articles 150 et suivants du Code Pénal".

VESSEL	:	"REGINA L."
LOADING PORT/BERTH	:	BATON ROUGE, LOUISIANA - U.S.A.
		AT SUPPLIERS SILO BATON ROUGE LA.
QUANTITY LOADED	:	52 996.999 Net Metric Tons (Of 1000 KG)
LOADING DATES	:	15 TO 16 TH SEPTEMBER 1993
BILL OF LADING	:	SEPTEMBER 16 TH 1993
COMMODITY DESCRIPTION	:	U.S. NO. 3 OR BETTER YELLOW CORN, IN BULK
SELLERS	:	TRADEXPORT
RECEIVERS	:	MINISTRY OF FOOD BANGLADESH
DESTINATION	:	PORT OF CHITTAGONG - BANGLADESH
L/C NO	:	677/93 DATED 2ND JUNE 1993
		CENTRAL BANK OF BANGLADESH, DACCA - BANGLADESH

Based on our inspection at time and place of loading, we hereby certify that we have supervised loading of the consignement in reference with the following results :

WEIGHT ASCERTAINEMENT : By checking automatic silo's weighing scales, weight loaded onboard was ascertained to be of **52 996.999 Net Metric Tons** (of 1 000 KG).

SAMPLING : Elementary sampling was carried out throughout loading operations every 500 MT and composited in sublot samples every 2500 MT loaded which were in turn mixed and divided to obtain representative samples intended to laboratory analyses.

QUALITY AND ANALYSIS : Analyses were performed on a representative sample by an independant laboratory and gave the following results which are in compliance with specifications and description of the goods as per relative L/C :

Quality and Grade : US N°3 or better YELLOW CORN
Moisture : 13.8 PCT (MAX 14.5 PCT).
Test Weight : 57.0 LBS/BUSHEL (MIN. 52 LBS/BUSHEL)
Broken kernels and Foreign Materials : 3.6 PCT (4 PCT MAX.)
Heat damaged kernels : 0.0 PCT (0.5 PCT MAX).
Total damaged kernels : 4.5 PCT (MAX 7PCT).
Aflatoxin compounds : 8.5 PPB (LESS THAN 10 PPB).

P.H. VITRAC
BUREAU VERITAS AGRI INSP DPT

Cette inspection a été effectuée dans le cadre des conditions générales du Bureau Veritas, elle ne dégage pas le vendeur de ses obligations contractuelles envers l'acheteur.
This inspection has been carried out within the scope of Bureau Veritas General Conditions, it does not release the seller from his contractual obligations towards the buyer.

Rappel des articles 10 et 11 des conditions générales du BUREAU VERITAS au verso.
Reminder : articles 10 and 11 of the BUREAU VERITAS general conditions at the back.

Ad.ME 9613 a

6. Transport Documents

Many of the problems in Documentary Credit operations are associated with the transport document - more often than not because the Documentary Credit stipulates a kind of document which is not appropriate to the mode, or modes, of carriage which will be used.

The 1993 revision of UCP aims at a less troubled future by recognising and providing distinct Articles covering different modes of transport.
(See **UCP 500 Articles 23, 24, 25, 26 27,28,29 and 30**).

Marine/ocean/port-to-port bill of lading

UCP 500 Article 23 covers in detail the requirements of a marine/ocean bill of lading covering a port-to-port shipment for presentation under a Documentary Credit.

The Article states that banks will accept such a document, however named, which:

- appears on its face to indicate the name of the carrier and to have been signed or otherwise authenticated by the carrier or the master or by a named agent for or on behalf of the carrier or the master,
- indicates that the goods have been loaded on board or shipped on a named vessel,
- indicates the port of loading and the port of discharge stipulated in the Documentary Credit,
- consists of a sole original or if issued in more than one original, the full set so issued,
- appears to contain all of the terms and conditions of carriage or some of such terms and conditions by reference to a source or document other than the bill of lading (short form/blank back bill of lading). Banks will not examine the contents of such terms and conditions,
- contains no indication that it is subject to a charter party and/or no indication that the carrying vessel is propelled by sail only,
- complies with the requirements of the Credit, and
- complies with the transhipment requirements as stated in **UCP 500 sub-Article 23 (b)(c)(d)**.

Specimen of a marine/ocean/port-to-port bill of lading

Bill of Lading

NEPTUNE ORIENT LINES LIMITED
HEAD OFFICE:
456 Alexandra Road,
#06-00 NOL Building,
Singapore 0511

NOL

SHIPPER / EXPORTER (COMPLETE NAME AND ADDRESS)	BOOKING NO.	BILL OF LADING NO.
	EXPORT REFERENCES	
CONSIGNEE (COMPLETE NAME AND ADDRESS)	FORWARDING AGENT, F.M.C. NO.	
	POINT AND COUNTRY OF ORIGIN OF GOODS	
NOTIFY PARTY (COMPLETE NAME AND ADDRESS)	ALSO NOTIFY - ROUTING & INSTRUCTIONS	

LOCAL VESSEL (WHEN TRANSHIPMENT IS INVOLVED)*	PLACE OF RECEIPT BY PRE-CARRIER*	
OCEAN VESSEL / VESSEL VOY FLAG	PORT OF LOADING	LOADING PIER / TERMINAL
PORT OF DISCHARGE	PLACE OF DELIVERY BY ON CARRIER*	FINAL DESTINATION (FOR MERCHANTS REFERENCE ONLY)

PARTICULARS FURNISHED BY SHIPPER

MARKS & NOS / CONTAINER NOS.	NO. OF PKGS	DESCRIPTION OF PACKAGES AND GOODS	GROSS WEIGHT LBS / KGS	MEASUREMENT M^3
		" S A M P L E "		

CHECKS IN PAYMENT OF FREIGHT AND OTHER CHARGES FOR THIS BILL OF LADING COLLECTABLE IN THE U.S.A. AND CANADA MUST BE PAID TO THE ORDER OF NEPTUNE ORIENT LINES LTD.

SHIPPERS DECLARED VALUE $
SUBJECT TO EXTRA FREIGHT AS PER TARIFF AND CARRIER'S LIABILITY LIMITS.

*APPLICABLE ONLY WHEN USED AS THROUGH BILL OF LADING.

FREIGHT & CHARGES	BASIS	RATE	PREPAID	COLLECT
			TOTAL	TOTAL

Received by the Carrier from the Shipper in apparent good order and condition (unless otherwise noted herein) the total number of Containers or other packages or units enumerated above and said by the Shipper to contain the Goods specified above (weight, quantity, contents, condition, quality and value unknown) for Carriage, subject to all the terms hereof (INCLUDING THE TERMS ON THE REVERSE HEREOF AND THE TERMS OF THE CARRIER'S APPLICABLE TARIFF) from the Place of Receipt or the Port of Loading, whichever is applicable, to the Place of Delivery or Port of Discharge, whichever is applicable. The Merchant in accepting this Bill of Lading or in presenting it to the Carrier expressly accepts and agrees to all its terms, conditions and exceptions, whether printed, stamped, or written or otherwise incorporated, notwithstanding the non-signing of this Bill of Lading by the Merchant.

FOR OTHER TERMS AND CONDITIONS SEE REVERSE SIDE

IN WITNESS WHEREOF the Master or Agent of said vessel hath affirmed to _____ Bills of Lading, all of this tenor and date, one of which being accomplished, the other(s) to stand void.
DATED
AT _____ ON _____

BY _____
As Agent
FOR: NEPTUNE ORIENT LINES LIMITED, As Carrier

Please note that this type of document must be issued, signed or authenticated as required in **UCP 500, article 23.**

Non-negotiable sea waybill

UCP 500 Article 24 covers in detail the requirements of a non-negotiable sea waybill covering a port-to-port shipment for presentation under a Documentary Credit.

The Article states that banks will accept such a document, however named, which:

- appears on its face to indicate the name of the carrier and to have been signed or otherwise authenticated by the carrier or the master or by a named agent for or on behalf of the carrier or the master,
- indicates that the goods have been loaded on board or shipped on a named vessel,
- indicates the port of loading and the port of discharge stipulated in the Documentary Credit,
- consists of a sole original, or if issued in more than one original, the full set so issued,
- appears to contain all of the terms and conditions of carriage or some of such terms and conditions by reference to a source or document other than the non-negotiable sea waybill (short form/blank back non-negotiable sea waybill). Banks will not examine the contents of such terms and conditions,
- contains no indication that it is subject to a charter party and/or no indication that the carrying vessel is propelled by sail only, and
- complies with the requirements of the Credit,
- complies with the transhipment requirements as stated in **UCP 500 sub-Articles 24 (b)(c)(d)**.

Specimen of a non-negotiable sea waybill

Non-Negotiable Waybill for Combined Transport shipment or Port to Port shipment

Shipper	Waybill No.
	Booking Ref.:
	Shipper's Ref.:

P&O
Containers

(Incorporating the business of ASSOCIATED CONTAINER TRANSPORTATION (Australia) LTD, and THE SHIPPING CORPORATION OF NEW ZEALAND LTD).

Consignee

Notify Party/Address (It is agreed that no responsibility shall attach to the Carrier or his Agents for failure to notify of the arrival of the goods)

Place of Receipt (Applicable only when this document is used as a Combined Transport Waybill)

Vessel and Voy. No.

Place of Delivery (Applicable only when this document is used as a Combined Transport Waybill)

Port of Loading

Port of Discharge

Marks and Nos; Container Nos;	Number and kind of Packages; description of Goods	Gross Weight (kg)	Measurement (cbm)

WAYBILL

Above particulars as declared by Shipper, but not acknowledged by the Carrier

★Total No. of Containers/Packages received by the Carrier

Received by the Carrier from the Shipper in apparent good order and condition (unless otherwise noted herein) the total number or quantity of Containers or other packages or units indicated in the box opposite entitled "*Total No. of Containers/Packages received by the Carrier" for Carriage from the Place of Receipt or the Port of Loading, whichever is applicable, to the Port of Discharge or the Place of Delivery, whichever applicable. SUBJECT TO THE TERMS OF THE CARRIER'S STANDARD BILL OF LADING TERMS AND CONDITIONS AND TARIFF FOR THE RELEVANT TRADE, WHICH ARE MUTATIS MUTANDIS APPLICABLE TO THIS WAYBILL (copies of which may be obtained from the Carrier or his agent). Except for live animals and Goods which are stated herein to be carried on deck and are so carried, these terms and conditions are warranted by the Carrier in respect of the sea portion of the Carriage to apply the Hague Rules or Hague Visby Rules, whichever would have been applicable if this Waybill were a Bill of Lading. In either case the provisions of Article III Rule 4 of the Hague Visby Rules are deemed to be incorporated herein.

The contract evidenced by this Waybill is deemed to be a contract of carriage as defined in Article 1(b) of the Hague Rules and Hague Visby Rules. However this Waybill is not a document of title to the Goods.

Delivery will be made to the Consignee named, or his authorised agent, on production of proof of identity at the Port of Discharge or the Place of Delivery, whichever applicable. Should the Consignee require delivery to a party and/or premises other than as shown above in the "Consignee" box, then written instructions must be given by the Consignee to the Carrier or his agent. Unless the Shipper expressly waives his right to control the Goods until delivery by means of a clause on the face hereof, such instructions from the Consignee will be subject to any instruction to the contrary by the Shipper.

Unless instructed to the contrary by the Shipper prior to the commencement of Carriage and noted accordingly on the face hereof, the Carrier will, subject to the aforesaid terms and conditions, process cargo claims with the Consignee. Claims settlement, if any, shall be a complete discharge of the Carrier's liability to the Shipper. The Shipper accepts the said standard terms and conditions on his own behalf, on behalf of the Consignee and the Owner of the Goods, and authorises the Consignee to bring suit against the Carrier in his own name but as agent of the Shipper, and warrants that he has authority so to accept and authorise. The Shipper further undertakes that no claim or allegation in respect of the Goods shall be made against the Carrier by any person other than in accordance with the terms and conditions of this Waybill.

Movement

Freight and Charges (indicate whether prepaid or collect):

Origin Inland Haulage Charge   ...   .

Origin Terminal Handling/LCL Service Charge   ...

Ocean Freight   ...   .

Destination Terminal Handling/LCL Service Charge ...

Destination Inland Haulage Charge   ...   .

Place and Date of Issue

IN WITNESS whereof this Waybill is signed

For P&O Containers Ltd as Carrier

ICS
C/T W/B
April 78

This Waybill is issued subject to the CMI Uniform Rules for Sea Waybills.

SHIPPED ON BOARD PER

OCEAN VESSEL ....

AT.................ON...................

FOR P&O CONTAINERS LTD.

P&O CONTAINERS LTD, Beagle House, Braham Street, London E1 8EP

ANZ WB2 11/92

P&O
Containers
As Agent(s) only.

046011   ....

Charter party bill of lading

UCP 500 Article 25 covers in detail the particulars of the charter party bill of lading and the requirements for presentation under a Documentary Credit.

If a Documentary Credit calls for or permits a charter party bill of lading, banks will, unless otherwise stipulated in the Documentary Credit, accept a bill of lading, however named, which:

- contains any indication that it is subject to a charter party,
- appears on its face to have been signed or otherwise authenticated by the master or by the owner, or by a named agent for or on behalf of the master or the owner,
- unless otherwise stipulated in the Documentary Credit, does not indicate the name of the carrier,
- indicates that the goods have been loaded on board or shipped on a named vessel,
- indicates the port of loading and the port of discharge stipulated in the Documentary Credit,
- consists of a sole original bill of lading, or if issued in more than one original, the full set as so issued, and
- contains no indication that the carrying vessel is propelled by sail only.

Specimen of a charter party bill of lading

| CODE NAME: "CEMENTVOYBILL" | BILL OF LADING | B/L No. | Page 2 |

Shipper

Reference No.

Consignee

Notify address

| Vessel | Port of loading |

Port of discharge

Shipper's description of cargo | Gross weight

Issued pursuant to
CHARTER-PARTY dated ....

Freight payable in accordance therewith.

FREIGHT ADVANCE.
Received on account of freight:

....

SHIPPED at the Port of Loading in apparent good order and condition on board the Vessel for carriage to the Port of Discharge or so near thereto as she may safely get the goods specified above.

Weight, measure, quality, quantity, condition, contents and value unknown.

IN WITNESS whereof the Master or Agent of the said Vessel has signed the number of Bills of Lading indicated below all of this tenor and date, any of which being accomplished the others shall be void.

FOR CONDITIONS OF CARRIAGE SEE OVERLEAF

| Freight payable at | Place and date of issue |

| Number of original Bs/L | Signature |

Printed and sold by
Fr. G. Knudtzons Bogtrykkeri A/S, 55 Toldbodgade, DK-1253 Copenhagen K,
by authority of The Baltic and International Maritime Council (BIMCO),
Copenhagen, Copyright.

Please note that this type of document must be issued, signed or authenticated as required in **UCP 500, article 25.**

Multimodal transport document

UCP 500 Article 26 covers in detail the requirements of a transport document covering at least two different modes of transport (multimodal transport) for presentation under a Documentary Credit.

It states that banks will accept such a document, however named, which:

- appears on its face to indicate the name of the carrier or multimodal transport operator and to have been signed or otherwise authenticated by the carrier or multimodal transport operator, the master, or a named agent for or on behalf of the carrier, multimodal transport operator or the master,
- indicates that the goods have been dispatched, taken in charge or loaded on board,
- indicates a place of taking in charge stipulated in the Documentary Credit which may be different from the port, airport or place of loading, and a place of final destination stipulated in the Documentary Credit which may be different from the port of discharge,
- consists of a sole original multimodal transport document, or if issued in more than one original, the full set as so issued,
- appears to contain the terms and conditions of carriage or merely contains some or all of such conditions by reference to a source or document other than the multimodal transport document (short form/blank back multimodal transport document). Banks will not examine the contents of such terms and conditions,
- contains no indication that it is subject to a charter party and/or no indication that the carrying vessel is propelled by sail only,
- in all other respects meets the stipulations of the Credit.

Specimen of a multimodal transport document

Bill of Lading
For Multimodal Transport or Port to Port Shipment

Page 2

Hapag-Lloyd

Shipper:	**Hapag-Lloyd Reference** / **B/L-No.**
	Export References
Consignee:	**Forwarding Agent**
	Consignee's Reference
Notify Address (Carrier not responsible for failure to notify; see clause 20 [1] hereof):	**Place of Receipt** (Applicable only when document used for **Multimodal** transport):
Pre-Carriage by: / **Place of Receipt by Pre-Carrier:**	**Place of Delivery** (Applicable only when document used for **Multimodal** transport):
Ocean Vessel: / **Port of Loading:**	
Port of Discharge: / **Place of Delivery by On-Carrier:**	

Container Nos., Seal Nos.; Marks and Nos.	Number and Kind of Packages; Description of Goods	Gross Weight (kg)	Measurement (cbm)

COPY

Above Particulars as Declared by Shipper

Total No. Containers/Packages received by the Carrier:		Shipper's declared value (see Clause 7 [3] hereof):				
Movement		Currency				
Charge	Rate	Basis	WT/MEA/VAL	Payment		Amount

Received by the Carrier from the Shipper in apparent good order and condition (unless otherwise noted herein) the total number or quantity of Containers or other packages or units indicated in the box opposite entitled "*Total No. of Containers/Packages received by the Carrier" for Carriage subject to all the terms and conditions hereof (**Including the Terms and Conditions on the Reverse hereof and the Terms and Conditions of the Carrier's Applicable Tariff**) from the Place of Receipt or the Port of Loading, whichever is applicable, to the Port of Discharge or the Place of Delivery, whichever is applicable. One original Bill of Lading, duly endorsed, must be surrendered by the Merchant to the Carrier in exchange for the Goods or a delivery order. In accepting this Bill of Lading the Merchant expressly accepts and agrees to all its terms and conditions whether printed, stamped or written, or otherwise incorporated, notwithstanding the non-signing of this Bill of Lading by the Merchant.

In Witness whereof the number of original Bills of Lading stated below all of this tenor and date has been signed, one of which being accomplished the others to stand void.

No. Original	Place and Date of Issue
Freight Payable at	For the Carrier
Loading Pier / Terminal	

Total Freight Prepaid	Total Freight Collect	Total Freight

90101926

Please note that this type of document must be issued, signed or authenticated as required in **UCP 500, article 26.**

Air transport document

UCP 500 Article 27 covers in detail the requirements of an air transport document for presentation under a Documentary Credit.

The Article states that banks will accept such a document, however named, which:

- appears on its face to indicate the name of the carrier and to have been signed or otherwise authenticated by the carrier or a named agent for or on behalf of the carrier,
- indicates that the goods have been accepted for carriage,
- indicates the actual date of dispatch when so required by the Documentary Credit, or if the actual date of dispatch is not required by the Documentary Credit, the date of issuance of the air transport document will be deemed to be the date of shipment,
- indicates the airports of departure and destination,
- appears to be the original for the consignor/shipper even if the Documentary Credit stipulates a full set of originals, or similar expressions,
- appears to contain all of the terms and conditions of carriage, or some of such terms and conditions, by reference to a source or document other than the air transport document,
- in all other respects meets the stipulations of the Credit, and
- complies with the transhipment requirements as stated in **UCP 500 sub-Articles 27(b)(c)**.

Specimen of an air transport document

Shipper's Name and Address		Shipper's Account Number	Not Negotiable
			Air Waybill
			Issued by

Copies 1, 2 and 3 of this Air Waybill are originals and have the same validity.

Consignee's Name and Address	

It is agreed that the goods described herein are accepted in apparent good order and condition (except as noted) for carriage SUBJECT TO THE CONDITIONS OF CONTRACT ON THE REVERSE HEREOF. ALL GOODS MAY BE CARRIED BY ANY OTHER MEANS INCLUDING ROAD OR ANY OTHER CARRIER UNLESS SPECIFIC CONTRARY INSTRUCTIONS ARE GIVEN HEREON BY THE SHIPPER. THE SHIPPER'S ATTENTION IS DRAWN TO THE NOTICE CONCERNING CARRIER'S LIMITATION OF LIABILITY. Shipper may increase such limitation of liability by declaring a higher value for carriage and paying a supplemental charge if required.

Issuing Carrier's Agent Name and City

Accounting Information

Agent's IATA Code	Account No.

Airport of Departure (Addr. of First Carrier) and Requested Routing

To	By First Carrier	Routing and Destination	to	by	to	by	Currency	WT/VAL		Other		Declared Value for Carriage	Declared Value for Customs
								PPD	COLL	PPD	COLL		

Airport of Destination			Amount of Insurance	INSURANCE — If carrier offers insurance, and such insurance is requested in accordance with the conditions thereof, indicate amount to be insured in figures in box marked "Amount of Insurance".

Handling Information

No. of Pieces RCP	Gross Weight	kg / lb	Rate Class / Commodity Item No.	Chargeable Weight	Rate / Charge	Total	Nature and Quantity of Goods (incl. Dimensions or Volume)

Prepaid	Weight Charge	Collect	Other Charges
	Valuation Charge		
	Tax		
	Total Other Charges Due Agent		Shipper certifies that the particulars on the face hereof are correct and that **insofar as any part of the consignment contains dangerous goods, such part is properly described by name and is in proper condition for carriage by air according to the applicable Dangerous Goods Regulations.**
	Total Other Charges Due Carrier		
			Signature of Shipper or his Agent
Total Prepaid	Total Collect		
			Executed on (date) at (place) Signature of Issuing Carrier or its Agent

ORIGINAL 3 (FOR SHIPPER)

Please note that this type of document must be issued, signed or authenticated as required in **UCP 500, article 27.**

Road, rail, or inland waterway transport document

UCP 500 Article 28 covers in detail the requirements of a road, rail or inland waterway transport document for presentation under a Documentary Credit.

The Article states that banks will accept such a document, however named, which:

- appears on its face to indicate the name of the carrier,
- bears a signature or other authentication and/or reception stamp or other indication of receipt by the carrier or a named agent for or on behalf of the carrier,
- indicates that the goods have been received for shipment, dispatch or carriage or wording to this effect,
- indicates the place of shipment and the place of destination as stipulated in the Credit,
- in the absence of any indication on the transport document as to the numbers issued, banks will accept the transport document(s) presented as constituting a full set. Banks will accept as original(s) the transport document(s) whether marked as original(s) or not,
- in all other respects meets the stipulations of the Credit, and
- complies with the transhipment requirements as stated in **UCP 500 sub-Articles 28(c)(d)**.

Specimen of a road transport document

1 Exemplaire de l'**expéditeur**
Copy for **sender**

1 Expéditeur (nom, adresse, pays)
Sender (name, address, country)

LETTRE DE VOITURE INTERNATIONALE
INTERNATIONAL CONSIGNMENT NOTE — No 24382

CMR

Ce transport est soumis, nonobstant toute clause contraire, à la Convention relative au contrat de transport international de marchandises par route (CMR).

This carriage is subject, notwithstanding any clause to the contrary, to the Convention on the Contract for the International Carriage of goods by road (CMR).

2 Destinataire (nom, adresse, pays)
Consignee (name, address, country)

16 Transporteur (nom, adresse, pays)
Carrier (name, address, country)

3 Lieu prévu pour la livraison de la marchandise (lieu, pays)
Place of delivery of the goods (place, country)

17 Transporteurs successifs (nom, adresse, pays)
Successive carriers (name, address, country)

4 Lieu et date de la prise en charge de la marchandise (lieu, pays, date)
Place and date of taking over the goods (place, country, date)

18 Réserves et observations du transporteur
Carrier's reservations and observations

5 Documents annexés
Documents attached

*Les parties encadrées de lignes grasses doivent être remplies par le transporteur
The spaces framed with heavy lines must be filled in by the carrier*

6 Marques et numéros Marks and Nos	**7** Nombre des colis Number of packages	**8** Mode d'emballage Method of packing	**9** Nature de la marchandise Nature of the goods	**10** No statistique Statistical number	**11** Poids brut, kg Gross weight in kg	**12** Cubage m3 Volume in m3

19 + 21 + 22.
*y compris et
Including and*

Classe Class	Chiffre Number	Lettre Letter	(ADR *)

1 – 15

*A remplir sous la responsabilité de l'expéditeur
To be completed on the sender's responsibility*

13 Instructions de l'expéditeur
Sender's instructions

19 Conventions particulières
Special agreements

20 À payer par To be paid by :	Expéditeur Senders	Monnaie/Currency	Destinataire Consignee
Prix de transport Carriage charges :			
Réductions Deductions : —			
Solde / Balance			
Suppléments Supplem. charges :			
Frais accessoires Other charges : +			
TOTAL :			

14 Prescriptions d'affranchissement
Instructions as to payment for carriage

☐ Franco / Carriage paid

☐ Non franco / Carriage forward

21 Etablie à
Established in — le / on — 19

15 Remboursement / Cash on delivery

22

23

24 Marchandises reçues / Goods received

Lieu
Place — le / on — 19

Signature et timbre de l'expéditeur
Signature and stamp of the sender

Signature et timbre du transporteur
Signature and stamp of the carrier

Signature et timbre du destinataire
Signature and stamp of the consignee

Modèle IRU 1976

*• En cas de marchandises dangereuses indiquer, outre la certification éventuelle, à la dernière ligne du cadre : la classe, le chiffre et le cas échéant, la lettre.
• In case of dangerous goods mention, besides the possible certification, on the last line of the column the particulars of the class, the number and the letter ; if any*

Specimen of a rail transport document

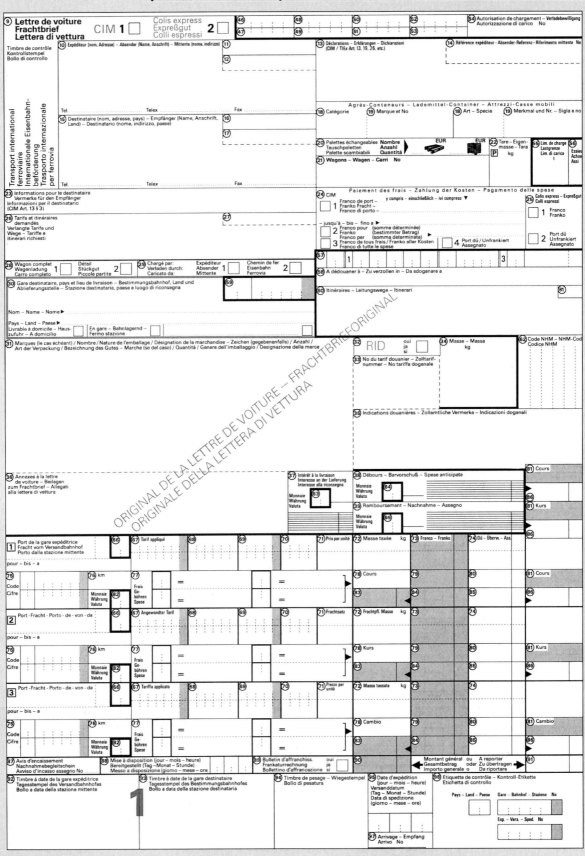

Courier and post receipt

UCP 500 Article 29 covers in detail the requirements of a post receipt, certificate of posting, or a document issued by a courier or expedited delivery service for presentation under a Documentary Credit.

The Article states that banks will accept such a document, however named, which:

- for a post receipt: appears on its face to have been stamped or otherwise authenticated and dated in the place from which the Documentary Credit stipulates the goods are to be shipped or dispatched,
- for a courier or expedited delivery service document: evidences receipt of the goods for delivery provided it appears to indicate on its face the name of courier or service and it is stamped, signed or otherwise authenticated by such named courier or service, and
- indicates a date of pick-up or receipt or wording to this effect.

Specimen of a courier service document

DHL WORLDWIDE EXPRESS®	**Lettre de Transport Aérien** 507004993 (Non négociable)

Noter ce numéro en cas de réclamation

ORIGINE — **DESTINATION**

1 De (Expéditeur)
Compte n°
Nom de l'expéditeur (en lettres capitales)
Référence de l'expéditeur
Nom de la société — Les 12 premiers caractères figureront sur la facture
Adresse
Code postal — Téléphone / Télécopie / Télex (préciser)

2 A (Destinataire)
Nom de la société
Adresse de livraison (DHL ne peut pas livrer à une boîte postale)
Code postal — Pays
Personne à contacter (personne à qui livrer) — Téléphone / Télécopie / Télex (préciser)

3 Détails de l'expédition
Tous nos services et moyens de paiement ne sont pas disponibles dans tous les pays.

Services
- DOCUMENT EXPRESS INTL.
- COLIS EXPRESS INTL (service Colis)
- INTRA CE (libre circulation)
- EXPRESS DOCUMENT (maxi 150 gr.)
- NATIONAL
- WORLDMAIL Première classe / Deuxième classe (préciser)
- AUTRE SERVICE .... préciser

Frais de transport
Si laissé en blanc, l'expéditeur paye les frais de transport
- Expéditeur
- Espèces/Chèque/Carte de crédit
Pour les clients agréés seulement
- Accord External Billing
- Transport Collect

Assurance de l'envoi (voir au verso)
- OUI .... Montant assuré, indiquer la devise

Description complète de l'envoi

Service Colis Express International seulement
Joindre l'original et trois copies de la facture proforma ou commerciale
Valeur déclarée indiquer la devise — Numéro d'identification TVA de l'expéditeur
Numéro de tarif douanier — Numéro d'identification TVA du destinataire
Catégorie d'exportation — PERMANENTE — REPARATION/RETOUR — TEMPORAIRE
Charges des droits et taxes de douane. Si laissé en blanc, le destinataire paye les droits et taxes
- Destinataire — Expéditeur — Autre .... (Préciser le numéro de compte approuvé par la destination)

4 Dimensions et poids
Nombre de pièces — Poids
.... kg
Dimensions en cm l x L x H
x — x

Poids volumétrique/poids facturé
.... kg

CODES	FRAIS Services
	Spécial
	Assurance
	Autre/TVA

CODE DEVISE — TOTAL

NUMÉRO ÉTIQUETTE TRANSPORT COLLECT

DETAILS DE PAIEMENT
Chèque / Carte de crédit n°

Type — Expiration
Enlevé par
Numéro de la route
Heure
Date

Station d'origine

Printed by Proforms BV Heerhugowaard The Netherlands

5 Autorisation et signature de l'Expéditeur
Je / nous reconnaissons avoir pris connaissance des conditions générales de DHL, applicables au présent envoi, dont un résumé figure au verso, limitant notamment la responsabilité de DHL. La Convention de Varsovie peut aussi être applicable (voir au verso)
Je / nous avons pleinement connaissance que DHL ne prend en charge ni monnaie fiduciaire, ni marchandise dangereuse (voir au verso)
Signature — Date / /

DHL INTERNATIONAL - Société Anonyme au capital de 87 000 000 FF - Z.I. PARIS NORD II - 161, rue de la Belle Etoile - BP 50252 - 95957 ROISSY CEDEX - R.C.S. PONTOISE: 334 834 033 (00139) - Identifiant TVA: CE FR 84 334 834 033

Transport document issued by freight forwarders

UCP 500 Article 30 covers in detail the conditions under which banks will accept a transport document issued by a freight forwarder.

Specimen of a transport document issued by a freight forwarder

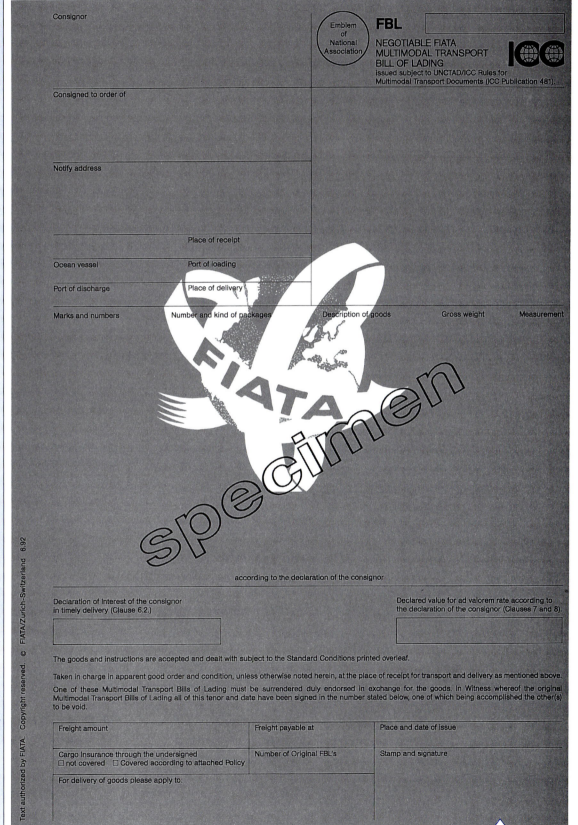

Consignor

Consigned to order of

Notify address

Emblem of National Association

FBL

NEGOTIABLE FIATA MULTIMODAL TRANSPORT BILL OF LADING
issued subject to UNCTAD/ICC Rules for Multimodal Transport Documents (ICC Publication 481).

ICC

Place of receipt

Ocean vessel | **Port of loading**

Port of discharge | **Place of delivery**

Marks and numbers | **Number and kind of packages** | **Description of goods** | **Gross weight** | **Measurement**

according to the declaration of the consignor

Declaration of interest of the consignor in timely delivery (Clause 6.2.)

Declared value for ad valorem rate according to the declaration of the consignor (Clauses 7 and 8).

The goods and instructions are accepted and dealt with subject to the Standard Conditions printed overleaf.

Taken in charge in apparent good order and condition, unless otherwise noted herein, at the place of receipt for transport and delivery as mentioned above.

One of these Multimodal Transport Bills of Lading must be surrendered duly endorsed in exchange for the goods. In Witness whereof the original Multimodal Transport Bills of Lading all of this tenor and date have been signed in the number stated below, one of which being accomplished the other(s) to be void.

Freight amount	Freight payable at	Place and date of issue
Cargo Insurance through the undersigned ☐ not covered ☐ Covered according to attached Policy	Number of Original FBL's	Stamp and signature
For delivery of goods please apply to:		

Text authorized by FIATA. Copyright reserved. © FIATA/Zurich-Switzerland 6.92

If this document is to be used other than as a freight forwarder transport document, it must be issued, signed or authenticated as required in **UCP 500, article 26.**

Specimen of a transport document issued by a freight forwarder

REGIONAL FREIGHT SERVICES   BILL OF LADING

SHIPPER/EXPORTER	DOCUMENT No.
	EXPORT REFERENCES
CONSIGNEE	FORWARDING AGENT—REFERENCES
NOTIFY PARTY	

Norwich and Head Office: Regional House,
Norwich Airport, Norwich NR6 6JA.
Telephone: (0603) 414125
Fax: (0603) 402542

| Bristol | Heathrow | Birmingham | Stansted | Gt. Yarmouth |
| 0934 863300 | 081 844 2203 | 021 782 3699 | 0279 681580 | 0493 331000 |

PLACE OF RECEIPT	CONTAINER No.	FOR PARTICULARS OF DELIVERY PLEASE APPLY WITH THIS B/L TO:
OCEAN VESSEL (Exporting Carrier)	PORT OF LOADING	
PORT OF DISCHARGE	FINAL DESTINATION	

PARTICULARS FURNISHED BY SHIPPER

MARKS AND NUMBERS	No. OF PKGS.	DESCRIPTION OF PACKAGES AND GOODS	GROSS WEIGHT	MEASUREMENT

CHARGED ON	ITEM	RATE	PER	PREPAID	COLLECT
TERMINALS					
CURRENCY ADJUSTMENT					
BUNKER SURCHARGE					
ADVANCE CHARGES COLLECT					
FREIGHT PAYABLE AT:	TOTAL CHARGES				

IN ACCEPTING THIS BILL OF LADING, the Shipper, Consignee, Holder hereof, and Owner of the goods, agree to be bound by all of its stipulations, exceptions and conditions, whether written, printed or stamped on the front or back hereof, as well as the provisions of the above Carrier's published Tariff Rules and Regulations, as fully as if they were all signed by such Shipper, Consignee, Holder or Owner, and it is further agreed that Containers may be stowed on Deck.
IN WITNESS WHEREOF, the Carrier or its Agent has affirmed to all of this tenor and date, ONE of which being accomplished, the others to stand void.

SIGNATURE FOR AND ON BEHALF OF

REGIONAL FREIGHT SERVICES

By _____

PLACE: DATE OF ISSUE:
No. OF ORIGINAL BILL OF LADING.

Terms of Bill of Landing continued on reverse side

If this document is to be used other than as a freight forwarder transport document, it must be issued, signed or authenticated as required in **UCP 500, articles 23 and 26.**

VI. *Settlement*

Settlement

1.

The seller sends the documents evidencing the shipment to the bank where the Credit is available (the nominated bank)

2.

After checking that the documents meet the Credit requirements, the bank makes payment

3.

This bank then sends the documents to the Issuing Bank

4.

The Issuing Bank, after checking that the documents meet the Credit requirements, makes reimbursement in the pre-agreed manner (see UCP 500 Article 19)

5.

The Issuing Bank then sends the Documents to the Buyer

6.

Reimbursement is obtained in the pre-agreed manner

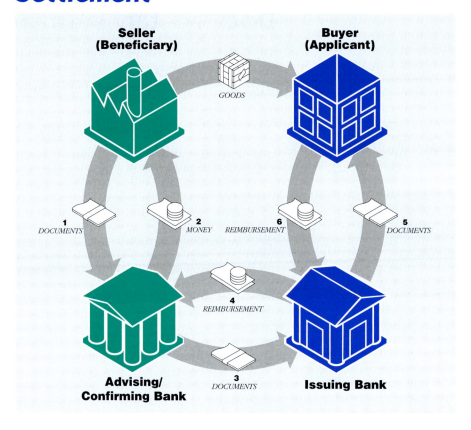

1. If the Documents do not meet the Documentary Credit Requirements

The seller may sometimes present documents that do not meet the Documentary Credit requirements. In such a case, the Confirming Bank or a Nominated Bank can only act in one of the following ways:

(a)   return all the documents to the presenter (the Beneficiary if presented directly by him or to his bankers or to any other party acting on his behalf) for correction and resubmission within the validity of the Documentary Credit and within the period of time after the date of shipment specified in the Documentary Credit or applicable under **UCP 500 sub-Article 43(a)**,

(b)   return just the discrepant document as in (a) above and safe-keep the remaining documents for the account of and on behalf of the presenter.

■ upon authorisation by the presenter, forward the discrepant documents on "an approval" basis under the Documentary Credit to the respective Issuing Bank for review and approval or rejection of the documents,

■ return all the documents to the presenter for direct action by him,

■ if so authorised by the presenter, cable, telex or telecommunicate with the Issuing Bank for authority to pay, accept, or negotiate against such discrepant documents,

■ accept an indemnity from the Beneficiary or his bankers, as appropriate, i.e. to pay, accept, or negotiate on the understanding that any payment, acceptance, or negotiation made will be refunded by the party giving such indemnity, together with interest and related charges, if the Issuing Bank refuses to take up the discrepant documents and refuses to provide reimbursement,

■ based on practical experience and with the agreement of the Beneficiary, pay, accept, or negotiate "under reserve", i.e. the bank retains the right of recourse against the Beneficiary if the Issuing Bank refuses to provide reimbursement against documents that do not meet the Documentary Credit requirements.

2. Types of Settlement

Settlement by payment

1.

The seller sends the documents evidencing the shipment to the bank where the Credit is available (the nominated bank)

2.

After checking that the documents meet the Credit requirements, the bank makes payment

3.

This bank then sends the documents to the Issuing Bank

4.

The Issuing Bank, after checking that the documents meet the Credit requirements, makes reimbursement in the pre-agreed manner (see UCP 500 Article 19)

5.

The Issuing Bank then sends the Documents to the Buyer

6.

Reimbursement is obtained in the pre-agreed manner

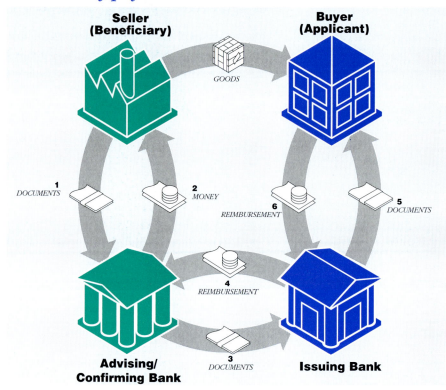

Settlement by acceptance

1.

The seller sends the documents evidencing the shipment to the bank where the Credit is available (the accepting bank) accompanied by a Draft drawn on the bank with the specified tenor

2.

After checking that the documents meet the Credit requirements, the bank accepts the Draft and returns it to the seller

3.

The Accepting Bank then sends the documents to the Issuing Bank, stating that it has accepted the Draft

4.

The Issuing Bank, after checking that the documents meet the Credit requirements, makes at maturity reimbursement in the pre-agreed manner

5.

The Issuing Bank then sends the Documents to the Buyer

6.

Reimbursement is obtained in the pre-agreed manner

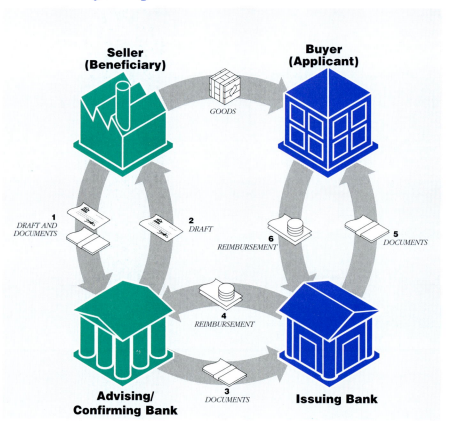

1.

The seller presents the Draft and documents evidencing shipment to the bank where the Credit is available for negotiation (the Negotiating Bank)

2.

After checking that the documents meet the Credit requirements, the Negotiating Bank remits the funds to the Beneficiary

3.

The Negotiating Bank then sends the Draft and documents to the Issuing Bank

4.

The Issuing Bank, after checking that the Draft and documents meet the Credit requirements, makes reimbursement in the pre-agreed manner

5.

The Issuing Bank then sends the documents to the Buyer

6.

Reimbursement is obtained in the pre-agreed manner

Settlement by negotiation

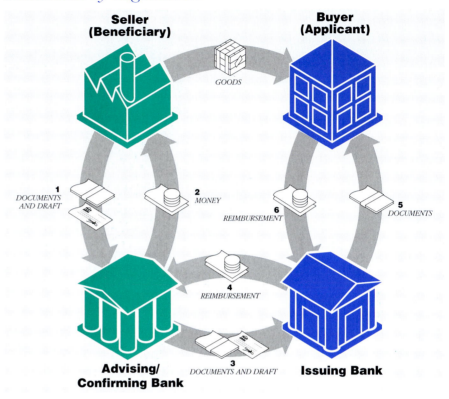

VII. Summary of Procedure and Check-list of Documents

1. Summary of Procedure

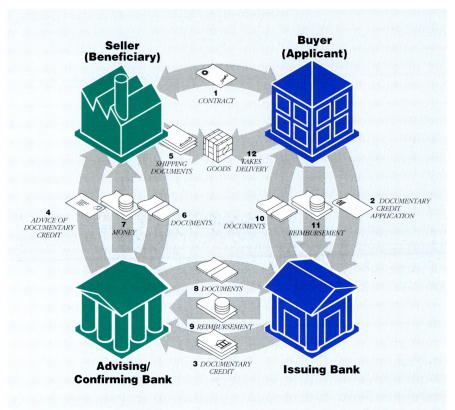

1.

The buyer and seller conclude a sales contract providing for payment by a Documentary Credit

2.

The buyer instructs his bank - the "Issuing Bank" - to issue a Documentary Credit in favour of the seller (Beneficiary)

3.

The Issuing Bank issues the Documentary Credit and asks another bank (the Advising Bank), usually in the country of the seller, to advise or confirm the Documentary Credit

4.

The Advising Bank informs the seller that the Documentary Credit has been issued

5.

As soon as the seller receives the Documentary Credit and is satisfied that it meets the terms of the sales contract and that he can meet the Documentary Credit terms and conditions, he is in a position to effect shipment

6.

Seller then sends the required documents to the bank where the Documentary Credit is made available (the Nominated Bank)

7.

The bank examines the documents against the Documentary Credit. If they meet the requirements of the Documentary Credit, the bank will pay, accept, or negotiate, according to the terms of the Documentary Credit

8.

The bank which takes up the documents sends the documents to the Issuing Bank

9.

The Issuing Bank examines the documents and, if the documents meet the Documentary Credit requirements, reimburses in the pre-agreed manner the Confirming Bank or any other Nominated Bank that has paid, accepted, or negotiated under the Documentary Credit

10.

When the documents have been examined by the Issuing Bank and are found to meet the Documentary Credit requirements, they are released to the buyer

11.

The Issuing Bank obtains reimbursement from the Buyer in the pre-agreed manner

12.

The buyer forwards the transport document to the local office or agent of the carrier who will then effect delivery of the goods to him

2. Suggested Checklist for Document Preparation and Examination

The reader should appreciate that this list is not exhaustive but is offered as a general guide to help in the preparation and examination of documents that could be required by the Documentary Credit.

It is not to be construed as being other than solely for guidance and there should be no legal imputation attached to it.

For the bank which receives the documents:

1.   The letter of transmittal

Ensure:

- ✔ that it is addressed to your bank,

- ✔ that it has a current date,

- ✔ that it relates to the Documentary Credit number referenced,

- ✔ that the documents enumerated are attached,

- ✔ that the value of the documents and the value mentioned in the cover letter are the same,

- ✔ that the bank (if any) remitting the documents is acting as a Paying, Accepting, Negotiating, or Remitting Bank,

- ✔ that the payment instructions are clear and understood,

- ✔ whether any discrepancy(ies) have been noted and whether payment, acceptance, or negotiation was effected against an indemnity or under reserve.

For the bank and the Beneficiary:

2.   The Documentary Credit

Ensure:

- ✔ that it is the correct referenced Documentary Credit,

- ✔ that it is still valid (not expired/cancelled),

- ✔ that the available balance in the Documentary Credit is sufficient to cover the value of the drawing,

- ✔ that the documents required by the Documentary Credit are presented,

- ✔ that no amendments or previous drawdowns are in a questionable state.

3. The draft

Ensure:

☑ that the Draft bears the correct Documentary Credit reference number,

☑ that it has a current date,

☑ that the signature and/or the name of the Drawer corresponds with the name of the Beneficiary,

☑ that it is drawn on the correct Drawee,

☑ that the amount in figures and words correspond,

☑ that the tenor is as required by the Documentary Credit,

☑ that the name of the payee is identified,

☑ that if it requires an endorsement it is properly endorsed,

☑ that there are no restricted endorsements,

☑ that it contains any necessary clauses as required by the Documentary Credit,

☑ that the amount drawn for does not exceed the balance available in the Documentary Credit,

☑ that the value of the draft and the invoices corresponds,

☑ that it is not drawn "without recourse" unless authorised by the Documentary Credit.

For the bank and the Beneficiary:

4. The invoice

Ensure:

☑ that it is issued by the Beneficiary of the Documentary Credit,

☑ that the Applicant (the buyer) is indicated as the invoiced party, unless otherwise stated in the Documentary Credit,

☑ that it is not titled "pro-forma" or "provisional" invoice,

☑ that the description of the goods corresponds with the merchandise description in the Documentary Credit,

☑ that no additional detrimental description of the goods appears that may question their condition or value,

☑ that the details of the goods, prices, and terms as mentioned in the Documentary Credit are included in the invoice,

✔ that any other information supplied in the invoice, such as marks, numbers, transportation information, etc. it is consistent with that of the other documents,

✔ that the currency of the invoice is the same as that of the Documentary Credit,

✔ that the value of the invoice corresponds with that of the Draft,

✔ that the value of the invoice does not exceed the available balance of the Documentary Credit,

✔ that the invoice covers the complete shipment as required by the Documentary Credit (if no part shipments are allowed),

✔ that if required by the Documentary Credit the invoice is signed, notarised, legalised, certified, etc.,

✔ that the information relative to the shipment, packaging, weight, freight charges or other related transport charges corresponds with that appearing on the other documents,

✔ that the correct number of original(s) and copy(ies) is presented.

For the bank and the Beneficiary

5. Other documents

Certificate of origin

Ensure:

✔ that it is a unique document and not combined with any other document,

✔ that it is signed, notarised, legalised, visaed as required by the Documentary Credit,

✔ that the data on it is consistent with that of the other documents,

✔ that the country of origin is specified, and that it meets the requirements of the Documentary Credit.

Weight list/certificate

Ensure:

✔ that it is a unique document and not combined with any other document,

✔ that it is signed if a certificate is called for, or as otherwise stated in the Documentary Credit,

✔ that the data on it is consistent with that of the other documents.

Packing list

Ensure:

 that it is a unique document and not combined with any other document,

 that it corresponds with the requirements of the Documentary Credit. A detailed packing list requires a listing of the contents of each package, carton, etc. and other relevant information,

 that the data on it is consistent with that of the other documents.

Inspection certificate

Ensure:

 that the inspection firm nominated in the Documentary Credit, if any, issued the certificate,

 that it is signed,

 that the certificate complies with the inspection requirements of the Documentary Credit,

 that it contains no detrimental statement as to the goods, specifications, quality, packaging, etc. unless authorised by the Documentary Credit,

Other miscellaneous documents

 UCP 500 Article 21 states:

"When documents other than transport documents, insurance documents and commercial invoices are called for, the Credit should stipulate by whom such documents are to be issued and their wording or data content. If the Credit does not so stipulate, banks will accept such documents as presented, provided that their data content is not inconsistent with any other stipulated document presented."

It should be noted that when Documentary Credits require a document to be issued as a "certificate", the document must be signed.

For the bank and the Beneficiary:

6. Insurance document

Ensure:

 that the policy/certificate/declaration/cover note, as required by the Documentary Credit, is presented,

 that the full set of the insurance document issued is presented,

 that it is issued and signed by the insurance company or underwriter or their agents, and the assured, if so required by the insurance document,

✔ that the date of issuance or date from which cover is effective at the latest from the date of loading on board or dispatch or taking in charge of the goods, as the case may be,

✔ that the value of the goods insured is as required by the Documentary Credit or as defined in **UCP 500 sub-Article 34(f)**,

✔ that it is issued in the same currency as the Documentary Credit, unless otherwise allowed in the Documentary Credit,

✔ that the goods description corresponds with that of the invoice,

✔ that it covers the merchandise from the designated port of embarkation or point of taking in charge to port of discharge or point of delivery,

✔ that it covers the specified risks as stated in the Documentary Credit and that the risks are clearly defined,

✔ that the marks and numbers, etc. correspond with those of the transport document,

✔ that if the assured named is other than the Confirming Bank, Issuing Bank or buyer, it bears the appropriate endorsement,

✔ that all other information appearing on the document is consistent with that of the other documents,

✔ that if any alteration is noted in the document it is properly authenticated.

For the bank and the Beneficiary:

7. Transport documents
Ensure

✔ that the full set of originals issued is presented,

✔ that it is not a "charter party" transport document, unless authorised in the Documentary Credit.

✔ that it is not a forwarder's transport document unless it is authorised in the Documentary Credit under **UCP 500 Article 30**,

✔ that the name of the consignee is as required in the Documentary Credit,

✔ that if the transport document requires endorsement it is appropriately endorsed,

✔ that it bears the name of the shipper or his agent,

✔ that the name and address, if any, of the notifying party is as required in the Documentary Credit,

✔ that the description of the goods generally corresponds to the description of the goods as stated in the Documentary Credit, and that the marks and numbers as well as other specifications, if any, are identical to those appearing on the other documents,

✔ that the indication of freight prepaid or freight collect costs, as required by the terms of the Documentary Credit, appears on it,

✔ that there are no clauses on the transport document that may render it "foul" or "unclean" (See **UCP 500 sub-Article 32(a)**),

✔ that all other conditions stipulated in the appropriate transport Articles of UCP 500 are complied with.

Appendices

ICC Uniform Customs and Practice for Documentary Credits (UCP 500)

A. General Provisions and Definitions

Article 1
Application of UCP

The Uniform Customs and Practice for Documentary Credits, 1993 Revision, ICC Publication N°500, shall apply to all Documentary Credits (including to the extent to which they may be applicable, Standby Letter(s) of Credit) where they are incorporated into the text of the Credit. They are binding on all parties thereto, unless otherwise expressly stipulated in the Credit.

Article 2
Meaning of Credit

For the purposes of these Articles, the expressions "Documentary Credit(s)" and "Standby Letter(s) of Credit" (hereinafter referred to as "Credit(s)"), mean any arrangement, however named or described, whereby a bank (the "Issuing Bank") acting at the request and on the instructions of a customer (the "Applicant") or on its own behalf,

i. is to make a payment to or to the order of a third party (the "Beneficiary"), or is to accept and pay bills of exchange (Draft(s)) drawn by the Beneficiary,

or
ii. authorises another bank to effect such payment, or to accept and pay such bills of exchange (Draft(s)),

or
iii. authorises another bank to negotiate, against stipulated document(s),provided that the terms and conditions of the Credit are complied with.

For the purposes of these Articles, branches of a bank in different countries are considered another bank.

Article 3
Credits v. Contracts

a Credits, by their nature, are separate transactions from the sales or other contract(s) on which they may be based and banks are in no way concerned with or bound by such contract(s), even if any reference whatsoever to such contract(s) is included in the Credit. Consequently, the undertaking of a bank to pay, accept and pay Draft(s) or negotiate and/or to fulfill any other obligation under the Credit, is not subject to claims or defences by the Applicant resulting from his relationships with the Issuing Bank or the Beneficiary.

b A Beneficiary can in no case avail himself of the contractual relationships existing between the banks or between the Applicant and the Issuing Bank.

Article 4
Documents v. Goods/Services/Performances

In Credit operations all parties concerned deal with documents, and not with goods, services and/or other performances to which the documents may relate.

Article 5
Instructions to Issue/Amend Credits

a Instructions for the issuance of a Credit, the Credit itself, instructions for an amendment thereto, and the amendment itself, must be complete and precise.

In order to guard against confusion and misunderstanding, banks should discourage any attempt:

i. to include excessive detail in the Credit or in any amendment thereto;

ii. to give instructions to issue, advise or confirm a Credit by reference to a Credit previously issued (similar Credit) where such previous Credit has been subject to accepted amendment(s), and/or unaccepted amendment(s).

b All instructions for the issuance of a Credit and the Credit itself and, where applicable, all instructions for an amendment thereto and the amendment itself, must state precisely the document(s) against which payment, acceptance or negotiation is to be made.

B. Form and Notification of Credits

Article 6
Revocable v. Irrevocable Credits

a A Credit may be either
i. revocable,

or
ii. irrevocable.

b The Credit, therefore, should clearly indicate whether it is revocable or irrevocable.

c In the absence of such indication the Credit shall be deemed to be irrevocable.

Article 7
Advising Bank's Liability

a A Credit may be advised to a Beneficiary through another bank (the "Advising Bank") without engagement on the part of the Advising Bank, but that bank, if it elects to advise the Credit, shall take reasonable care to check the apparent authenticity of the Credit which it advises. If the bank elects not to advise the Credit, it must so inform the Issuing Bank without delay.

b If the Advising Bank cannot establish such apparent authenticity it must inform, without delay, the bank from which the instructions appear to have been received that it has been unable to establish the authenticity of the Credit and if it elects nonetheless to advise the Credit it must inform the Beneficiary that it has not been able to establish the authenticity of the Credit.

Article 8
Revocation of a Credit

a A revocable Credit may be amended or cancelled by the Issuing Bank at any moment and without prior notice to the Beneficiary.

b However, the Issuing Bank must:

i. reimburse another bank with which a revocable Credit has been made available for sight payment, acceptance or negotiation – for any payment, acceptance or negotiation made by such bank – prior to receipt by it of notice of amendment or cancellation, against documents which appear on their face to be in compliance with the terms and conditions of the Credit;

ii. reimburse another bank with which a revocable Credit has been made available for deferred payment, if such a bank has, prior to receipt by it of notice of amendment or cancellation, taken up documents which appear on their face to be in compliance with the terms and conditions of the Credit.

Article 9
Liability of Issuing and Confirming Banks

a An irrevocable Credit constitutes a definite undertaking of the Issuing Bank, provided that the stipulated documents are presented to the Nominated Bank or to the Issuing Bank and that the terms and conditions of the Credit are complied with:

i. if the Credit provides for sight payment – to pay at sight;

ii. if the Credit provides for deferred payment – to pay on the maturity date(s) determinable in accordance with the stipulations of the Credit;

iii. if the Credit provides for acceptance:

a. by the Issuing Bank – to accept Draft(s) drawn by the Beneficiary on the Issuing Bank and pay them at maturity,

or
b. by another drawee bank – to accept and pay at maturity Draft(s) drawn by the Beneficiary on the Issuing Bank in the event the drawee bank stipulated in the Credit does not accept Draft(s) drawn on it, or to pay Draft(s) accepted but not paid by such drawee bank at maturity;

iv. if the Credit provides for negotiation – to pay without recourse to drawers and/or bona fide holders, Draft(s) drawn by the Beneficiary and/or document(s) presented under the Credit. A Credit should not be issued available by Draft(s) on the Applicant. If the Credit nevertheless calls for Draft(s) on the Applicant, banks will consider such Draft(s) as an additional document(s).

b A confirmation of an irrevocable Credit by another bank (the "Confirming Bank") upon the authorisation or request of the Issuing Bank, constitutes a definite undertaking of the Confirming Bank, in addition to that of the Issuing Bank, provided that the stipulated documents are presented to the Confirming Bank or to any other Nominated Bank and that the terms and conditions of the Credit are complied with:

i. if the Credit provides for sight payment – to pay at sight;

ii. if the Credit provides for deferred payment – to pay on the maturity date(s) determinable in accordance with the stipulations of the Credit;

iii. if the Credit provides for acceptance:

a. by the Confirming Bank – to accept Draft(s) drawn by the Beneficiary on the Confirming Bank and pay them at maturity,
or
b. by another drawee bank – to accept and pay at maturity Draft(s) drawn by the Beneficiary on the Confirming Bank, in the event the drawee bank stipulated in the Credit does not accept Draft(s) drawn on it, or to pay Draft(s) accepted but not paid by such drawee bank at maturity;

iv. if the Credit provides for negotiation – to negotiate without recourse to drawers and/or bona fide holders, Draft(s) drawn by the Beneficiary and/or document(s) presented under the Credit.

A Credit should not be issued available by Draft(s) on the Applicant. If the Credit nevertheless calls for Draft(s) on the Applicant, banks will consider such Draft(s) as an additional document(s).

c   **i.** If another bank is authorised or requested by the Issuing Bank to add its confirmation to a Credit but is not prepared to do so, it must so inform the Issuing Bank without delay.

    ii. Unless the Issuing Bank specifies otherwise in its authorisation or request to add confirmation, the Advising Bank may advise the Credit to the Beneficiary without adding its confirmation.

d   **i.** Except as otherwise provided by Article 48, an irrevocable Credit can neither be amended nor cancelled without the agreement of the Issuing Bank, the Confirming Bank, if any, and the Beneficiary.

    ii. The Issuing Bank shall be irrevocably bound by an amendment(s) issued by it from the time of the issuance of such amendment(s). A Confirming Bank may extend its confirmation to an amendment and shall be irrevocably bound as of the time of its advice of the amendment. A Confirming Bank may, however, choose to advise an amendment to the Beneficiary without extending its confirmation and, if so, must inform the Issuing Bank and the Beneficiary without delay.

    iii. The terms of the original Credit (or a Credit incorporating previously accepted amendment(s)) will remain in force for the Beneficiary until the Beneficiary communicates his acceptance of the amendment to the bank that advised such amendment. The Beneficiary should give notification of acceptance or rejection of amendment(s). If the Beneficiary fails to give such notification, the tender of documents to the Nominated Bank or Issuing Bank, that conform to the Credit and to not yet accepted amendment(s), will be deemed to be notification of acceptance by the Beneficiary of such amendment(s) and as of that moment the Credit will be amended.

    iv. Partial acceptance of amendments contained in one and the same advice of amendment is not allowed and consequently will not be given any effect.

Article 10
Types of Credit

a   All Credits must clearly indicate whether they are available by sight payment, by deferred payment, by acceptance or by negotiation.

b   **i.** Unless the Credit stipulates that it is available only with the Issuing Bank, all Credits must nominate the bank (the "Nominated Bank") which is authorised to pay, to incur a deferred payment undertaking, to accept Draft(s) or to negotiate. In a freely negotiable Credit, any bank is a Nominated Bank.
Presentation of documents must be made to the Issuing Bank or the Confirming Bank, if any, or any other Nominated Bank.

    ii. Negotiation means the giving of value for Draft(s) and/or document(s) by the bank authorised to negotiate. Mere examination of the documents without giving of value does not constitute a negotiation.

c   Unless the Nominated Bank is the Confirming Bank, nomination by the Issuing Bank does not constitute any undertaking by the Nominated Bank to pay, to incur a deferred payment undertaking, to accept Draft(s), or to negotiate. Except where expressly agreed to by the Nominated Bank and so communicated to the Beneficiary, the Nominated Bank's receipt of and/or examination and/or forwarding of the documents does not make that bank liable to pay, to incur a deferred payment undertaking, to accept Draft(s), or to negotiate.

d   By nominating another bank, or by allowing for negotiation by any bank, or by authorising or requesting another bank to add its confirmation, the Issuing Bank authorises such bank to pay, accept Draft(s) or negotiate, as the case may be, against documents which appear on their face to be in compliance with the terms and conditions of the Credit and undertakes to reimburse such bank in accordance with the provisions of these Articles.

Article 11
Teletransmitted and Pre-Advised Credits

a   **i.** When an Issuing Bank instructs an Advising Bank by an authenticated teletransmission to advise a Credit or an amendment to a Credit, the teletransmission will be deemed to be the operative Credit instrument or the operative amendment, and no mail confirmation should be sent. Should a mail confirmation nevertheless be sent, it will have no effect and the Advising Bank will have no obligation to check such mail confirmation against the operative Credit instrument or the operative amendment received by teletransmission.

    ii. If the teletransmission states "full details to follow" (or words of similar effect) or states that the mail confirmation is to be the operative Credit instrument or the operative amendment, then the teletransmission will not be deemed to be the operative Credit instrument or the operative amendment. The Issuing Bank must forward the operative Credit instrument or the operative amendment to such Advising Bank without delay.

b   If a bank uses the services of an Advising Bank to have the Credit advised to the Beneficiary, it must also use the services of the same bank for advising an amendment(s).

c   A preliminary advice of the issuance or amendment of an irrevocable Credit (pre-advice), shall only be given by an Issuing Bank if such bank is prepared to issue the operative Credit instrument or the operative amendment thereto. Unless otherwise stated in such preliminary advice by the Issuing Bank, an Issuing Bank having given such pre-advice shall be irrevocably committed to issue or amend the Credit, in terms not inconsistent with the pre-advice, without delay.

Article 12
Incomplete or Unclear Instructions

If incomplete or unclear instructions are received to advise, confirm or amend a Credit, the bank requested to act on such instructions may give preliminary notification to the Beneficiary for information only and without responsibility. This preliminary notification should state clearly that the notification is provided for information only and without the responsibility of the Advising Bank. In any event, the Advising Bank must inform the Issuing Bank of the action taken and request it to provide the necessary information.

The Issuing Bank must provide the necessary information without delay. The Credit will be advised, confirmed or amended only when complete and clear instructions have been received and if the Advising Bank is then prepared to act on the instructions.

C. Liabilities and Responsibilities

Article 13
Standard for Examination of Documents

a   Banks must examine all documents stipulated in the Credit with reasonable care, to ascertain whether or not they appear, on their face, to be in compliance with the terms and conditions of the Credit. Compliance of the stipulated documents on their face with the terms and conditions of the Credit shall be determined by international standard banking practice as reflected in these Articles. Documents which appear on their face to be inconsistent with one another will be considered as not appearing on their face to be in compliance with the terms and conditions of the Credit.

Documents not stipulated in the Credit will not be examined by banks. If they receive such documents, they shall return them to the presenter or pass them on without responsibility.

b   The Issuing Bank, the Confirming Bank, if any, or a Nominated Bank acting on their behalf, shall each have a reasonable time, not to exceed seven banking days following the day of receipt of the documents, to examine the documents and determine whether to take up or refuse the documents and to inform the party from which it received the documents accordingly.

c   If a Credit contains conditions without stating the document(s) to be presented in compliance therewith, banks will deem such conditions as not stated and will disregard them.

Article 14
Discrepant Documents and Notice

a   When the Issuing Bank authorises another bank to pay, incur a deferred payment undertaking, accept Draft(s), or negotiate against documents which appear on their face to be in compliance with the terms and conditions of the Credit, the Issuing Bank and the Confirming Bank, if any, are bound:

    i. to reimburse the Nominated Bank which has paid, incurred a deferred payment undertaking, accepted Draft(s), or negotiated,

    ii. to take up the documents.

b   Upon receipt of the documents the Issuing Bank and/or Confirming Bank, if any, or a Nominated Bank acting on their behalf, must determine on the basis of the documents alone whether or not they appear on their face to be in compliance with the terms and conditions of the Credit. If the documents appear on their face not to be in compliance with the terms and conditions of the Credit, such banks may refuse to take up the documents.

c   If the Issuing Bank determines that the documents appear on their face not to be in compliance with the terms and conditions of the Credit, it may in its sole judgment approach the Applicant for a waiver of the discrepancy(ies). This does not, however, extend the period mentioned in sub-Article 13 (b).

d   **i.**   If the Issuing Bank and/or Confirming Bank, if any, or a Nominated Bank acting on their behalf, decides to refuse the documents, it must give notice to that effect by telecommunication or, if that is not possible, by other expeditious means, without delay but no later than the close of the seventh banking day following the day of receipt of the documents. Such notice shall be given to the bank from which it received the documents, or to the Beneficiary, if it received the documents directly from him.

   ii.   Such notice must state all discrepancies in respect of which the bank refuses the documents and must also state whether it is holding the documents at the disposal of, or is returning them to, the presenter.

   iii.   The Issuing Bank and/or Confirming Bank, if any, shall then be entitled to claim from the remitting bank refund, with interest, of any reimbursement which has been made to that bank.

e   If the Issuing Bank and/or Confirming Bank, if any, fails to act in accordance with the provisions of this Article and/or fails to hold the documents at the disposal of, or return them to the presenter, the Issuing Bank and/or Confirming Bank, if any, shall be precluded from claiming that the documents are not in compliance with the terms and conditions of the Credit.

f   If the remitting bank draws the attention of the Issuing Bank and/or Confirming Bank, if any, to any discrepancy(ies) in the document(s) or advises such banks that it has paid, incurred a deferred payment undertaking, accepted Draft(s) or negotiated under reserve or against an indemnity in respect of such discrepancy(ies), the Issuing Bank and/or Confirming Bank, if any, shall not be thereby relieved from any of their obligations under any provision of this Article. Such reserve or indemnity concerns only the relations between the remitting bank and the party towards whom the reserve was made, or from whom, or on whose behalf, the indemnity was obtained.

Article 15
Disclaimer on Effectiveness of Documents
Banks assume no liability or responsibility for the form, sufficiency, accuracy, genuineness, falsification or legal effect of any document(s), or for the general and/or particular conditions stipulated in the document(s) or superimposed thereon; nor do they assume any liability or responsibility for the description, quantity, weight, quality, condition, packing, delivery, value or existence of the goods represented by any document(s), or for the good faith or acts and/or omissions, solvency, performance or standing of the consignors, the carriers, the forwarders, the consignees or the insurers of the goods, or any other person whomsoever.

Article 16
Disclaimer on the Transmission of Messages
Banks assume no liability or responsibility for the consequences arising out of delay and/or loss in transit of any message(s), letter(s) or document(s), or for delay, mutilation or other error(s) arising in the transmission of any telecommunication. Banks assume no liability or responsibility for errors in translation and/or interpretation of technical terms, and reserve the right to transmit Credit terms without translating them.

Article 17
Force Majeure
Banks assume no liability or responsibility for the consequences arising out of the interruption of their business by Acts of God, riots, civil commotions, insurrections, wars or any other causes beyond their control, or by any strikes or lockouts. Unless specifically authorised, banks will not, upon resumption of their business, pay, incur a deferred payment undertaking, accept Draft(s) or negotiate under Credits which expired during such interruption of their business.

Article 18
Disclaimer for Acts of an Instructed Party
a   Banks utilizing the services of another bank or other banks for the purpose of giving effect to the instructions of the Applicant do so for the account and at the risk of such Applicant.

b   Banks assume no liability or responsibility should the instructions they transmit not be carried out, even if they have themselves taken the initiative in the choice of such other bank(s).

c   **i.**   A party instructing another party to perform services is liable for any charges, including commissions, fees, costs or expenses incurred by the instructed party in connection with its instructions.

   ii.   Where a Credit stipulates that such charges are for the account of a party other than the instructing party, and charges cannot be collected, the instructing party remains ultimately liable for the payment thereof.

d   The Applicant shall be bound by and liable to indemnify the banks against all obligations and responsibilities imposed by foreign laws and usages.

Article 19
Bank-to-Bank Reimbursement Arrangements
a   If an Issuing Bank intends that the reimbursement to which a paying, accepting or negotiating bank is entitled shall be obtained by such bank (the "Claiming Bank"), claiming on another party (the "Reimbursing Bank"), it shall provide such Reimbursing Bank in good time with the proper instructions or authorisation to honour such reimbursement claims.

b   Issuing Banks shall not require a Claiming Bank to supply a certificate of compliance with the terms and conditions of the Credit to the Reimbursing Bank.

c   An Issuing Bank shall not be relieved from any of its obligations to provide reimbursement if and when reimbursement is not received by the Claiming Bank from the Reimbursing Bank.

d   The Issuing Bank shall be responsible to the Claiming Bank for any loss of interest if reimbursement is not provided by the Reimbursing Bank on first demand, or as otherwise specified in the Credit, or mutually agreed, as the case may be.

e   The Reimbursing Bank's charges should be for the account of the Issuing Bank. However, in cases where the charges are for the account of another party, it is the responsibility of the Issuing Bank to so indicate in the original Credit and in the reimbursement authorisation. In cases where the Reimbursing Bank's charges are for the account of another party, they shall be collected from the Claiming Bank when the Credit is drawn under. In cases where the Credit is not drawn under, the Reimbursing Bank's charges remain the obligation of the Issuing Bank.

D. Documents

Article 20
Ambiguity as to the Issuers of Documents
a   Terms such as "first class", "well known", "qualified", "independent", "official", "competent", "local" and the like, shall not be used to describe the issuers of any document(s) to be presented under a Credit. If such terms are incorporated in the Credit, banks will accept the relative document(s) as presented, provided that it appears on its face to be in compliance with the other terms and conditions of the Credit and not to have been issued by the Beneficiary.

b   Unless otherwise stipulated in the Credit, banks will also accept as an original document(s), a document(s) produced or appearing to have been produced:

   i.   by reprographic, automated or computerized systems,

   ii.   as carbon copies,

   provided that it is marked as original and, where necessary, appears to be signed.

   A document may be signed by handwriting, by facsimile signature, by perforated signature, by stamp, by symbol, or by any other mechanical or electronic method of authentication.

c   **i.**   Unless otherwise stipulated in the Credit, banks will accept as a copy(ies), a document(s) either labelled copy or not marked as an original - a copy(ies) need not be signed.

   ii.   Credits that require multiple document(s) such as "duplicate", "two fold", "two copies" and the like, will be satisfied by the presentation of one original and the remaining number in copies except where the document itself indicates otherwise.

d   Unless otherwise stipulated in the Credit, a condition under a Credit calling for a document to be authenticated, validated, legalised, visaed, certified or indicating a similar requirement, will be satisfied by any signature, mark, stamp or label on such document that on its face appears to satisfy the above condition.

Article 21
Unspecified Issuers or Contents of Documents
When documents other than transport documents, insurance documents and commercial invoices are called for, the Credit should stipulate by whom such documents are to be issued and their wording or data content. If the Credit does not so stipulate, banks will accept such documents as presented, provided that their data content is not inconsistent with any other stipulated document presented.

Article 22
Issuance Date of Documents v. Credit Date
Unless otherwise stipulated in the Credit, banks will accept a document bearing a date of issuance prior to that of the Credit, subject to such document being presented within the time limits set out in the Credit and in these Articles.

Article 23
Marine/Ocean Bill of Lading
a If a Credit calls for a bill of lading covering a port-to-port shipment, banks will, unless otherwise stipulated in the Credit, accept a document, however named, which:

   i. appears on its face to indicate the name of the carrier and to have been signed or otherwise authenticated by:

     - the carrier or a named agent for or on behalf of the carrier, or

     - the master or a named agent for or on behalf of the master.

   Any signature or authentication of the carrier or master must be identified as carrier or master, as the case may be. An agent signing or authenticating for the carrier or master must also indicate the name and the capacity of the party, i.e. carrier or master, on whose behalf that agent is acting,

   and
   ii. indicates that the goods have been loaded on board, or shipped on a named vessel.

   Loading on board or shipment on a named vessel may be indicated by pre-printed wording on the bill of lading that the goods have been loaded on board a named vessel or shipped on a named vessel, in which case the date of issuance of the bill of lading will be deemed to be the date of loading on board and the date of shipment.

   In all other cases loading on board a named vessel must be evidenced by a notation on the bill of lading which gives the date on which the goods have been loaded on board, in which case the date of the on-board notation will be deemed to be the date of shipment.

   If the bill of lading contains the indication "intended vessel", or similar qualification in relation to the vessel, loading on-board a named vessel must be evidenced by an on board notation on the bill of lading which, in addition to the date on which the goods have been loaded on board, also includes the name of the vessel on which the goods have been loaded, even if they have been loaded on the vessel named as the "intended vessel".

   If the bill of lading indicates a place of receipt or taking in charge different from the port of loading, the on-board notation must also include the port of loading stipulated in the Credit and the name of the vessel on which the goods have been loaded, even if they have been loaded on the vessel named in the bill of lading. This provision also applies whenever loading on board the vessel is indicated by pre-printed wording on the bill of lading,

   and
   iii. indicates the port of loading and the port of discharge stipulated in the Credit, notwithstanding that it:

     a. indicates a place of taking in charge different from the port of loading, and/or a place of final destination different from the port of discharge,

     and/or
     b. contains the indication "intended" or similar qualification in relation to the port of loading and/or port of discharge, as long as the document also states the ports of loading and/or discharge stipulated in the Credit,

   and
   iv. consists of a sole original bill of lading or, if issued in more than one original, the full set as so issued,

   and
   v. appears to contain all of the terms and conditions of carriage, or some of such terms and conditions by reference to a source or document other than the bill of lading (short form/blank back bill of lading); banks will not examine the contents of such terms and conditions,

   and
   vi. contains no indication that it is subject to a charter party and/or no indication that the carrying vessel is propelled by sail only,

   and
   vii. in all other respects meets the stipulations of the Credit.

b For the purpose of this Article, transhipment means unloading and reloading from one vessel to another vessel during the course of ocean carriage from the port of loading to the port of discharge stipulated in the Credit.

c Unless transhipment is prohibited by the terms of the Credit, banks will accept a bill of lading which indicates that the goods will be transhipped, provided that the entire ocean carriage is covered by one and the same bill of lading.

d Even if the Credit prohibits transhipment, banks will accept a bill of lading which:
   i. indicates that transhipment will take place as long as the relevant cargo is shipped in Container(s), Trailer(s) and/or "LASH" barge(s) as evidenced by the bill of lading, provided that the entire ocean carriage is covered by one and the same bill of lading,

and/or
   ii. incorporates clauses stating that the carrier reserves the right to tranship.

Article 24
Non-Negotiable Sea Waybill
a If a Credit calls for a non-negotiable sea waybill covering a port-to-port shipment, banks will, unless otherwise stipulated in the Credit, accept a document, however named, which:

   i. appears on its face to indicate the name of the carrier and to have been signed or otherwise authenticated by:

     - the carrier or a named agent for or on behalf of the carrier, or

     - the master or a named agent for or on behalf of the master,

   Any signature or authentication of the carrier or master must be identified as carrier or master, as the case may be. An agent signing or authenticating for the carrier or master must also indicate the name and the capacity of the party, i.e. carrier or master, on whose behalf that agent is acting,

   and
   ii. indicates that the goods have been loaded on board, or shipped on a named vessel.

   Loading on board or shipment on a named vessel may be indicated by pre-printed wording on the non-negotiable sea waybill that the goods have been loaded on board a named vessel or shipped on a named vessel, in which case the date of issuance of the non-negotiable sea waybill will be deemed to be the date of loading on board and the date of shipment.

   In all other cases loading on board a named vessel must be evidenced by a notation on the non-negotiable sea waybill which gives the date on which the goods have been loaded on-board, in which case the date of the on board notation will be deemed to be the date of shipment.

   If the non-negotiable sea waybill contains the indication "intended vessel", or similar qualification in relation to the vessel, loading on board a named vessel must be evidenced by an on-board notation on the non-negotiable sea waybill which, in addition to the date on which the goods have been loaded on board, includes the name of the vessel on which the goods have been loaded, even if they have been loaded on the vessel named as the "intended vessel".

   If the non-negotiable sea waybill indicates a place of receipt or taking in charge different from the port of loading, the on-board notation must also include the port of loading stipulated in the Credit and the name of the vessel on which the goods have been loaded, even if they have been loaded on a vessel named in the non-negotiable sea waybill. This provision also applies whenever loading on board the vessel is indicated by pre-printed wording on the non-negotiable sea waybill,

   and
   iii. indicates the port of loading and the port of discharge stipulated in the Credit, notwithstanding that it:

     a. indicates a place of taking in charge different from the port of loading, and/or a place of final destination different from the port of discharge,

     and/or
     b. contains the indication "intended" or similar qualification in relation to the port of loading and/or port of discharge, as long as the document also states the ports of loading and/or discharge stipulated in the Credit,

   and
   iv. consists of a sole original non-negotiable sea waybill, or if issued in more than one original, the full set as so issued,

   and
   v. appears to contain all of the terms and conditions of carriage, or some of such terms and conditions by reference to a source or document other than the non-negotiable sea waybill (short form/blank back non-negotiable sea waybill); banks will not examine the contents of such terms and conditions,

and
vi. contains no indication that it is subject to a charter party and/or no indication that the carrying vessel is propelled by sail only,

and
vii. in all other respects meets the stipulations of the Credit.

b For the purpose of this Article, transhipment means unloading and reloading from one vessel to another vessel during the course of ocean carriage from the port of loading to the port of discharge stipulated in the Credit.

c Unless transhipment is prohibited by the terms of the Credit, banks will accept a non-negotiable sea waybill which indicates that the goods will be transhipped, provided that the entire ocean carriage is covered by one and the same non-negotiable sea waybill.

d Even if the Credit prohibits transhipment, banks will accept a non-negotiable sea waybill which,

  i. indicates that transhipment will take place as long as the relevant cargo is shipped in Container(s), Trailer(s) and/or "LASH" barge(s) as evidenced by the non-negotiable sea waybill, provided that the entire ocean carriage is covered by one and the same non-negotiable sea waybill,

  and/or
  ii. incorporates clauses stating that the carrier reserves the right to tranship.

Article 25
Charter Party Bill of Lading
a If a Credit calls for or permits a charter party bill of lading, banks will, unless otherwise stipulated in the Credit, accept a document, however named, which,
  i. contains any indication that it is subject to a charter party,

  and
  ii. appears on its face to have been signed or otherwise authenticated by,

    - the master or a named agent for or on behalf of the master, or

    - the owner or a named agent for or on behalf of the owner.

    Any signature or authentication of the master or owner must be identified as master or owner as the case may be. An agent signing or authenticating for the master or owner must also indicate the name and the capacity of the party, i.e. master or owner, on whose behalf that agent is acting,

  and
  iii. does or does not indicate the name of the carrier,

  and
  iv. indicates that the goods have been loaded on board or shipped on a named vessel.

    Loading on board or shipment on a named vessel may be indicated by pre-printed wording on the bill of lading that the goods have been loaded on board a named vessel or shipped on a named vessel, in which case the date of issuance of the bill of lading will be deemed to be the date of loading on board and the date of shipment.

    In all other cases loading on board a named vessel must be evidenced by a notation on the bill of lading which gives the date on which the goods have been loaded on board, in which case the date of the on-board notation will be deemed to be the date of shipment,

  and
  v. indicates the port of loading and the port of discharge stipulated in the Credit,

  and
  vi. consists of a sole original bill of lading or, if issued in more than one original, the full set as so issued,

  and
  vii. contains no indication that the carrying vessel is propelled by sail only,

  and
  viii. in all other respects meets the stipulations of the Credit.

b Even if the Credit requires the presentation of a charter party contract in connection with a charter party bill of lading, banks will not examine such charter party contract, but will pass it on without responsibility on their part.

Article 26
Multimodal Transport Document
a If a Credit calls for a transport document covering at least two different modes of transport (multimodal transport), banks will, unless otherwise stipulated in the Credit, accept a document, however named, which,

  i. appears on its face to indicate the name of the carrier or multimodal transport operator and to have been signed or otherwise authenticated by:

    - the carrier or multimodal transport operator or a named agent for or on behalf of the carrier or multimodal transport operator,

    or
    - the master or a named agent for or on behalf of the master.

    Any signature or authentication of the carrier, multimodal transport operator or master must be identified as carrier, multimodal transport operator or master, as the case may be. An agent signing or authenticating for the carrier, multimodal transport operator or master must also indicate the name and the capacity of the party, i.e. carrier, multimodal transport operator or master, on whose behalf that agent is acting,

  and
  ii. indicates that the goods have been dispatched, taken in charge or loaded on board.

    Dispatch, taking in charge or loading on board may be indicated by wording to that effect on the multimodal transport document and the date of issuance will be deemed to be the date of dispatch, taking in charge or loading on board and the date of shipment. However, if the document indicates, by stamp or otherwise, a date of dispatch, taking in charge or loading on board, such date will be deemed to be the date of shipment,

  and
  iii. a. indicates the place of taking in charge stipulated in the Credit which may be different from the port, airport or place of loading, and the place of final destination stipulated in the Credit which may be different from the port, airport or place of discharge,

    and/or
    b. contains the indication "intended" or similar qualification in relation to the vessel and/or port of loading and/or port of discharge,

  and
  iv. consists of a sole original multimodal transport document or, if issued in more than one original, the full set as so issued,

  and
  v. appears to contain all of the terms and conditions of carriage, or some of such terms and conditions by reference to a source or document other than the multimodal transport document (short form/blank back multimodal transport document); banks will not examine the contents of such terms and conditions,

  and
  vi. contains no indication that it is subject to a charter party and/or no indication that the carrying vessel is propelled by sail only,

  and
  vii. in all other respects meets the stipulations of the Credit.

b Even if the Credit prohibits transhipment, banks will accept a multimodal transport document which indicates that transhipment will or may take place, provided that the entire carriage is covered by one and the same multimodal transport document.

Article 27
Air Transport Document
a If a Credit calls for an air transport document, banks will, unless otherwise stipulated in the Credit, accept a document, however named, which,
  i. appears on its face to indicate the name of the carrier and to have been signed or otherwise authenticated by:

    - the carrier, or

    - a named agent for or on behalf of the carrier.

    Any signature or authentication of the carrier must be identified as carrier. An agent signing or authenticating for the carrier must also indicate the name and the capacity of the party, i.e. carrier, on whose behalf that agent is acting,

  and
  ii. indicates that the goods have been accepted for carriage,

  and
  iii. where the Credit calls for an actual date of dispatch, indicates a specific notation of such date, the date of dispatch so indicated on the air transport document will be deemed to be the date of shipment.

    For the purpose of this Article, the information appearing in the box on the air transport document (marked "For Carrier Use Only" or similar expression) relative to the flight number and date will not be considered as a specific notation of such date of dispatch.

    In all other cases, the date of issuance of the air transport document will be deemed to be the date of shipment,

  and
  iv. indicates the airport of departure and the airport of destination stipulated in the Credit,

  and
  v. appears to be the original for consignor/shipper even if the Credit stipulates a full set of originals, or similar expressions,

and

vi. appears to contain all of the terms and conditions of carriage, or some of such terms and conditions, by reference to a source or document other than the air transport document; banks will not examine the contents of such terms and conditions,

and

vii. in all other respects meets the stipulations of the Credit.

b For the purpose of this Article, transhipment means unloading and reloading from one aircraft to another aircraft during the course of carriage from the airport of departure to the airport of destination stipulated in the Credit.

c Even if the Credit prohibits transhipment, banks will accept an air transport document which indicates that transhipment will or may take place, provided that the entire carriage is covered by one and the same air transport document.

Article 28
Road, Rail or Inland Waterway Transport Documents

a If a Credit calls for a road, rail, or inland waterway transport document, banks will, unless otherwise stipulated in the Credit, accept a document of the type called for, however named, which,

i. appears on its face to indicate the name of the carrier and to have been signed or otherwise authenticated by the carrier or a named agent for or on behalf of the carrier and/or to bear a reception stamp or other indication of receipt by the carrier or a named agent for or on behalf of the carrier.

Any signature, authentication, reception stamp or other indication of receipt of the carrier must be identified on its face as that of the carrier. An agent signing or authenticating for the carrier, must also indicate the name and the capacity of the party, i.e. carrier on whose behalf that agent is acting,

and

ii. indicates that the goods have been received for shipment, dispatch or carriage or wording to this effect. The date of issuance will be deemed to be the date of shipment unless the transport document contains a reception stamp, in which case the date of the reception stamp will be deemed to be the date of shipment,

and

iii. indicates the place of shipment and the place of destination stipulated in the Credit,

and

iv. in all other respects meets the stipulations of the Credit.

b In the absence of any indication on the transport document as to the numbers issued, banks will accept the transport document(s) presented as constituting a full set. Banks will accept as original(s) the transport document(s) whether marked as original(s) or not.

c For the purpose of this Article, transhipment means unloading and reloading from one means of conveyance to another means of conveyance, in different modes of transport, during the course of carriage from the place of shipment to the place of destination stipulated in the Credit.

d Even if the Credit prohibits transhipment, banks will accept a road, rail, or inland waterway transport document which indicates that transhipment will or may take place, provided that the entire carriage is covered by one and the same transport document and within the same mode of transport.

Article 29
Courier and Post Receipts

a If a Credit calls for a post receipt or certificate of posting, banks will, unless otherwise stipulated in the Credit, accept a post receipt or certificate of posting which,

i. appears on its face to have been stamped or otherwise authenticated and dated in the place from which the Credit stipulates the goods are to be shipped or dispatched and such date will be deemed to be the date of shipment or dispatch,

and

ii. in all other respects meets the stipulations of the Credit.

b If a Credit calls for a document issued by a courier or expedited delivery service evidencing receipt of the goods for delivery, banks will, unless otherwise stipulated in the Credit, accept a document, however named, which,

i. appears on its face to indicate the name of the courier/service, and to have been stamped, signed or otherwise authenticated by such named courier/service (unless the Credit specifically calls for a document issued by a named Courier/Service, banks will accept a document issued by any Courier/Service),

and

ii. indicates a date of pick-up or of receipt or wording to this effect, such date being deemed to be the date of shipment or dispatch,

and

iii. in all other respects meets the stipulations of the Credit.

Article 30
Transport Documents issued by Freight Forwarders

Unless otherwise authorised in the Credit, banks will only accept a transport document issued by a freight forwarder if it appears on its face to indicate:

i. the name of the freight forwarder as a carrier or multimodal transport operator and to have been signed or otherwise authenticated by the freight forwarder as carrier or multimodal transport operator,

or

ii. the name of the carrier or multimodal transport operator and to have been signed or otherwise authenticated by the freight forwarder as a named agent for or on behalf of the carrier or multimodal transport operator.

Article 31
On Deck, Shipper's Load and Count, Name of Consignor

Unless otherwise stipulated in the Credit, banks will accept a transport document which,

i. does not indicate, in the case of carriage by sea or by more than one means of conveyance including carriage by sea, that the goods are or will be loaded on deck. Nevertheless, banks will accept a transport document which contains a provision that the goods may be carried on deck, provided that it does not specifically state that they are or will be loaded on deck,

and/or

ii. bears a clause on the face thereof such as "shipper's load and count" or "said by shipper to contain" or words of similar effect,

and/or

iii. indicates as the consignor of the goods a party other than the Beneficiary of the Credit.

Article 32
Clean Transport Documents

a A clean transport document is one which bears no clause or notation which expressly declares a defective condition of the goods and/or the packaging.

b Banks will not accept transport documents bearing such clauses or notations unless the Credit expressly stipulates the clauses or notations which may be accepted.

c Banks will regard a requirement in a Credit for a transport document to bear the clause "clean on board" as complied with if such transport document meets the requirements of this Article and of Articles 23, 24, 25, 26, 27, 28 or 30.

Article 33
Freight Payable/Prepaid Transport Documents

a Unless otherwise stipulated in the Credit, or inconsistent with any of the documents presented under the Credit, banks will accept transport documents stating that freight or transportation charges (hereafter referred to as "freight") have still to be paid.

b If a Credit stipulates that the transport document has to indicate that freight has been paid or prepaid, banks will accept a transport document on which words clearly indicating payment or prepayment of freight appear by stamp or otherwise, or on which payment or prepayment of freight is indicated by other means. If the Credit requires courier charges to be paid or prepaid, banks will also accept a transport document issued by a courier or expedited delivery service evidencing that courier charges are for the account of a party other than the consignee.

c The words "freight prepayable" or "freight to be prepaid" or words of similar effect, if appearing on transport documents, will not be accepted as constituting evidence of the payment of freight.

d Banks will accept transport documents bearing reference by stamp or otherwise to costs additional to the freight, such as costs of, or disbursements incurred in connection with, loading, unloading or similar operations, unless the conditions of the Credit specifically prohibit such reference.

Article 34
Insurance Documents

a Insurance documents must appear on their face to be issued and signed by insurance companies or underwriters or their agents.

b If the insurance document indicates that it has been issued in more than one original, all the originals must be presented unless otherwise authorised in the Credit.

c Cover notes issued by brokers will not be accepted, unless specifically authorised in the Credit.

d Unless otherwise stipulated in the Credit, banks will accept an insurance certificate or a declaration under an open cover pre-signed by insurance companies or underwriters or their agents. If a Credit specifically calls for an insurance certificate or a declaration under an open cover, banks will accept, in lieu thereof, an insurance policy.

e Unless otherwise stipulated in the Credit, or unless it appears from the insurance document that the cover is effective at the latest from the date of loading on board or dispatch or taking in charge of the goods, banks will not accept an insurance document which bears a date of issuance later than the date of loading on board or dispatch or taking in charge as indicated in such transport document.

f i. Unless otherwise stipulated in the Credit, the insurance document must be expressed in the same currency as the Credit.

ii. Unless otherwise stipulated in the Credit, the minimum amount for which the insurance document must indicate the insurance cover to have been effected is the CIF (cost, insurance and freight (… "named port of destination")) or CIP (carriage and insurance paid to (…"named place of destination")) value of the goods, as the case may be, plus 10%, but only when the CIF or CIP value can be determined from the documents on their face. Otherwise, banks will accept as such minimum amount 110% of the amount for which payment, acceptance or negotiation is requested under the Credit, or 110% of the gross amount of the invoice, whichever is the greater.

Article 35
Type of Insurance Cover
a Credits should stipulate the type of insurance required and, if any, the additional risks which are to be covered. Imprecise terms such as "usual risks" or "customary risks" shall not be used; if they are used, banks will accept insurance documents as presented, without responsibility for any risks not being covered.

b Failing specific stipulations in the Credit, banks will accept insurance documents as presented, without responsibility for any risks not being covered.

c Unless otherwise stipulated in the Credit, banks will accept an insurance document which indicates that the cover is subject to a franchise or an excess (deductible).

Article 36
All-Risks Insurance Cover
Where a Credit stipulates "insurance against all risks", banks will accept an insurance document which contains any "all risks" notation or clause, whether or not bearing the heading "all risks", even if the insurance document indicates that certain risks are excluded, without responsibility for any risk(s) not being covered.

Article 37
Commercial Invoices
a Unless otherwise stipulated in the Credit, commercial invoices;

i. must appear on their face to be issued by the Beneficiary named in the Credit (except as provided in Article 48),

and
ii. must be made out in the name of the Applicant (except as provided in sub-Article 48 (h)),

and
iii. need not be signed.

b Unless otherwise stipulated in the Credit, banks may refuse commercial invoices issued for amounts in excess of the amount permitted by the Credit. Nevertheless, if a bank authorised to pay, incur a deferred payment undertaking, accept Draft(s), or negotiate under a Credit accepts such invoices, its decision will be binding upon all parties, provided that such bank has not paid, incurred a deferred payment undertaking, accepted Draft(s) or negotiated for an amount in excess of that permitted by the Credit.

c The description of the goods in the commercial invoice must correspond with the description in the Credit. In all other documents, the goods may be described in general terms not inconsistent with the description of the goods in the Credit.

Article 38
Other Documents
If a Credit calls for an attestation or certification of weight in the case of transport other than by sea, banks will accept a weight stamp or declaration of weight which appears to have been superimposed on the transport document by the carrier or his agent unless the Credit specifically stipulates that the attestation or certification of weight must be by means of a separate document.

E. Miscellaneous Provisions

Article 39
Allowances in Credit Amount, Quantity and Unit Price
a The words "about", "approximately", "circa" or similar expressions used in connection with the amount of the Credit or the quantity or the unit price stated in the Credit are to be construed as allowing a difference not to exceed 10% more or 10% less than the amount or the quantity or the unit price to which they refer.

b Unless a Credit stipulates that the quantity of the goods specified must not be exceeded or reduced, a tolerance of 5% more or 5% less will be permissible, always provided that the amount of the drawings does not exceed the amount of the Credit. This tolerance does not apply when the Credit stipulates the quantity in terms of a stated number of packing units or individual items.

c Unless a Credit which prohibits partial shipments stipulates otherwise, or unless sub-Article (b) above is applicable, a tolerance of 5% less in the amount of the drawing will be permissible, provided that if the Credit stipulates the quantity of the goods, such quantity of goods is shipped in full, and if the Credit stipulates a unit price, such price is not reduced. This provision does not apply when expressions referred to in sub-Article (a) above are used in the Credit.

Article 40
Partial Shipments/Drawings
a Partial drawings and/or shipments are allowed, unless the Credit stipulates otherwise.

b Transport documents which appear on their face to indicate that shipment has been made on the same means of conveyance and for the same journey, provided they indicate the same destination, will not be regarded as covering partial shipments, even if the transport documents indicate different dates of shipment and/or different ports of loading, places of taking in charge, or dispatch.

c Shipments made by post or by courier will not be regarded as partial shipments if the post receipts or certificates of posting or courier's receipts or dispatch notes appear to have been stamped, signed or otherwise authenticated in the place from which the Credit stipulates the goods are to be dispatched, and on the same date.

Article 41
Instalment Shipments/Drawings
If drawings and/or shipments by instalments within given periods are stipulated in the Credit and any instalment is not drawn and/or shipped within the period allowed for that instalment, the Credit ceases to be available for that and any subsequent instalments, unless otherwise stipulated in the Credit.

Article 42
Expiry Date and Place for Presentation of Documents
a All Credits must stipulate an expiry date and a place for presentation of documents for payment, acceptance, or with the exception of freely negotiable Credits, a place for presentation of documents for negotiation. An expiry date stipulated for payment, acceptance or negotiation will be construed to express an expiry date for presentation of documents.

b Except as provided in sub-Article 44(a), documents must be presented on or before such expiry date.

c If an Issuing Bank states that the Credit is to be available "for one month", "for six months", or the like, but does not specify the date from which the time is to run, the date of issuance of the Credit by the Issuing Bank will be deemed to be the first day from which such time is to run. Banks should discourage indication of the expiry date of the Credit in this manner.

Article 43
Limitation on the Expiry Date
a In addition to stipulating an expiry date for presentation of documents, every Credit which calls for a transport document(s) should also stipulate a specified period of time after the date of shipment during which presentation must be made in compliance with the terms and conditions of the Credit. If no such period of time is stipulated, banks will not accept documents presented to them later than 21 days after the date of shipment. In any event, documents must be presented not later than the expiry date of the Credit.

b In cases in which sub-Article 40(b) applies, the date of shipment will be considered to be the latest shipment date on any of the transport documents presented.

Article 44
Extension of Expiry Date
a If the expiry date of the Credit and/or the last day of the period of time for presentation of documents stipulated by the Credit or applicable by virtue of Article 43 falls on a day on which the bank to which presentation has to be made is closed for reasons other than those referred to in Article 17, the stipulated expiry date and/or the last day of the period of time after the date of shipment for presentation of documents, as the case may be, shall be extended to the first following day on which such bank is open.

b The latest date for shipment shall not be extended by reason of the extension of the expiry date and/or the period of time after the date of shipment for presentation of documents in accordance with sub-Article (a) above. If no such latest date for shipment is stipulated in the Credit or, amendments thereto, banks will not accept transport documents indicating a date of shipment later than the expiry date stipulated in the Credit or amendments thereto.

c The bank to which presentation is made on such first following business day must provide a statement that the documents were presented within the time limits extended in accordance with sub-Article 44(a) of the Uniform Customs and Practice for Documentary Credits, 1993 Revision, ICC Publication No. 500.

Article 45
Hours of Presentation

Banks are under no obligation to accept presentation of documents outside their banking hours.

Article 46
General Expressions as to Dates for Shipment

a Unless otherwise stipulated in the Credit, the expression "shipment" used in stipulating an earliest and/or a latest date for shipment will be understood to include expressions such as, "loading on board", "dispatch", "accepted for carriage", "date of post receipt", "date of pick-up", and the like, and in the case of a Credit calling for a multimodal transport document the expression "taking in charge".

b Expressions such as "prompt", "immediately", "as soon as possible", and the like should not be used. If they are used banks will disregard them.

c If the expression "on or about" or similar expressions are used, banks will interpret them as a stipulation that shipment is to be made during the period from five days before to five days after the specified date, both end days included.

Article 47
Date Terminology for Periods of Shipment

a The words "to", "until", "till", "from" and words of similar import applying to any date or period in the Credit referring to shipment will be understood to include the date mentioned.

b The word "after" will be understood to exclude the date mentioned.

c The terms "first half" and "second half" of a month shall be construed respectively as the 1st to the 15th, and the 16th to the last day of such month, all dates inclusive.

d The terms "beginning", "middle", or "end" of a month shall be construed respectively as the 1st to the 10th, the 11th to the 20th, and the 21st to the last day of such month, all dates inclusive.

F. Transferable Credit

Article 48
Transferable Credit

a A transferable Credit is a Credit under which the Beneficiary (First Beneficiary) may request the bank authorised to pay, incur a deferred payment undertaking, accept or negotiate (the "Transferring Bank"), or in the case of a freely negotiable Credit, the bank specifically authorised in the Credit as a Transferring Bank, to make the Credit available in whole or in part to one or more other Beneficiary(ies) (Second Beneficiary(ies)).

b A Credit can be transferred only if it is expressly designated as "transferable" by the Issuing Bank. Terms such as "divisible", "fractionable", "assignable", and "transmissible" do not render the Credit transferable. If such terms are used they shall be disregarded.

c The Transferring Bank shall be under no obligation to effect such transfer except to the extent and in the manner expressly consented to by such bank.

d At the time of making a request for transfer and prior to transfer of the Credit, the First Beneficiary must irrevocably instruct the Transferring Bank whether or not he retains the right to refuse to allow the Transferring Bank to advise amendments to the Second Beneficiary(ies). If the Transferring Bank consents to the transfer under these conditions, it must, at the time of transfer, advise the Second Beneficiary(ies) of the First Beneficiary's instructions regarding amendments.

e If a Credit is transferred to more than one Second Beneficiary(ies), refusal of an amendment by one or more Second Beneficiary(ies) does not invalidate the acceptance(s) by the other Second Beneficiary(ies) with respect to whom the Credit will be amended accordingly. With respect to the Second Beneficiary(ies) who rejected the amendment, the Credit will remain unamended.

f Transferring Bank charges in respect of transfers including commissions, fees, costs or expenses are payable by the First Beneficiary, unless otherwise agreed. If the Transferring Bank agrees to transfer the Credit, it shall be under no obligation to effect the transfer until such charges are paid.

g Unless otherwise stated in the Credit, a transferable Credit can be transferred once only. Consequently, the Credit cannot be transferred at the request of the Second Beneficiary to any subsequent Third Beneficiary. For the purpose of this Article, a retransfer to the First Beneficiary does not constitute a prohibited transfer.

Fractions of a transferable Credit (not exceeding in the aggregate the amount of the Credit) can be transferred separately, provided partial shipments/drawings are not prohibited, and the aggregate of such transfers will be considered as constituting only one transfer of the Credit.

h The Credit can be transferred only on the terms and conditions specified in the original Credit, with the exception of:
- the amount of the Credit,
- any unit price stated therein,
- the expiry date,
- the last date for presentation of documents in accordance with Article 43,
- the period for shipment,

any or all of which may be reduced or curtailed.

The percentage for which insurance cover must be effected may be increased in such a way as to provide the amount of cover stipulated in the original Credit, or these Articles.

In addition, the name of the First Beneficiary can be substituted for that of the Applicant, but if the name of the Applicant is specifically required by the original Credit to appear in any document(s) other than the invoice, such requirement must be fulfilled.

i The First Beneficiary has the right to substitute his own invoice(s) (and Draft(s)) for those of the Second Beneficiary(ies), for amounts not in excess of the original amount stipulated in the Credit and for the original unit prices if stipulated in the Credit, and upon such substitution of invoice(s) (and Draft(s)) the First Beneficiary can draw under the Credit for the difference, if any, between his invoice(s) and the Second Beneficiary's(ies') invoice(s).

When a Credit has been transferred and the First Beneficiary is to supply his own invoice(s) (and Draft(s)) in exchange for the Second Beneficiary's(ies') invoice(s) (and Draft(s)) but fails to do so on first demand, the Transferring Bank has the right to deliver to the Issuing Bank the documents received under the transferred Credit, including the Second Beneficiary's(ies') invoice(s) (and Draft(s)) without further responsibility to the First Beneficiary.

j The First Beneficiary may request that payment or negotiation be effected to the Second Beneficiary(ies) at the place to which the Credit has been transferred up to and including the expiry date of the Credit, unless the original Credit expressly states that it may not be made available for payment or negotiation at a place other than that stipulated in the Credit. This is without prejudice to the First Beneficiary's right to substitute subsequently his own invoice(s) (and Draft(s)) for those of the Second Beneficiary(ies) and to claim any difference due to him.

G. Assignment of Proceeds

Article 49
Assignment of Proceeds

The fact that a Credit is not stated to be transferable shall not affect the Beneficiary's right to assign any proceeds to which he may be, or may become, entitled under such Credit, in accordance with the provisions of the applicable law. This Article relates only to the assignment of proceeds and not to the assignment of the right to perform under the Credit itself.

ICC ARBITRATION

Contracting parties that wish to have the possibility of resorting to ICC Arbitration in the event of a dispute with their contracting partner should specifically and clearly agree upon ICC Arbitration in their contract, or, in the event no single contractual document exists, in the exchange of correspondence which constitutes the agreement between them. The fact of issuing a letter of credit subject to the UCP 500 does NOT by itself constitute an agreement to have resort to ICC Arbitration. The following standard arbitration clause is recommended by the ICC:

"All disputes arising in connection with the present contract shall be finally settled under the Rules of Conciliation and Arbitration of the International Chamber of Commerce by one or more arbitrators appointed in accordance with the said Rules".

THE ICC AT A GLANCE

Founded in 1919, the ICC is a non-governmental organisation of thousands of companies and business associations in more than 130 countries. ICC National Committees throughout the world present ICC views to their governments and alert Paris headquarters to national business concerns.

The ICC

- represents the world business community at national and international levels;
- promotes world trade and investment based on free and fair competition;
- harmonises trade practices and formulates terminology and guidelines for importers and exporters;
- provides a growing range of practical services to business.
- Through its subsidiary, ICC Publishing S.A., the ICC produces a wide range of publications. It also holds vocational seminars and business conferences in cities throughout the world.

Some ICC Services

The ICC International Court of Arbitration (Paris); The ICC International Centre for Expertise ; The ICC International Maritime Bureau (London); The ICC Centre for Maritime Co-operation (London); The ICC Counterfeiting Intelligence Bureau (London); The ICC Commercial Crime Bureau (London); The ICC International Bureau of Chambers of Commerce - IBCC (Paris); The ICC Institute of International Business Law and Practice (Paris); The ICC World Industry Council for the Environment - WICE (Paris).

SELECTED ICC PUBLICATIONS

DOCUMENTARY CREDITS

Documentary Credits UCP 500 and 400 Compared
Edited by Charles del Busto
| E | 148 pages · 21 x 29.7 cm | ISBN 92-842-1157-3 | N° 511 |

The New ICC Standard Documentary Credit Forms
Edited by Charles del Busto
| E | 80 pages · 21 x 29,7 cm | ISBN 92-842-1160-3 | N° 516 |

Uniform Customs and Practice for Documentary Credits (1993 Revision)
| E-F-ES-ED 60 pages · 10.5 x 21 cm | ISBN 92-842-1155-7 | N° 500 |
(other languages available)

BANKING AND FINANCE

Funds Transfer in International Banking
Edited by Charles del Busto
| E | 115 pages · 16 x 24 cm | ISBN 92-842-1128-X | N° 497 |

Guide to the ICC Uniform Rules for Demand Guarantees
by Roy Goode
| E | 140 pages · 16 x 24 cm | ISBN 92-842-1145-X | N° 510 |

HOW TO OBTAIN ICC PUBLICATIONS?

All ICC publications are available from ICC National Committees in some 60 countries, or from:

ICC Publishing S.A.
38, Cours Albert 1er
75008 Paris, France.
Customer Service:
Tel. (33 1) 49 53 29 23
Fax (33 1) 49 53 29 02

ICC Publishing Inc.
156 Fifth Avenue.
New York, N.Y. 10010
United States
Tel (212) 206 1150
Fax (212) 633 6025